M000281048

SO GOD MADE A MOTHER

SO GOD MADE A
mother

tender, proud, strong, faithful, known, beautiful,
worthy & unforgettable—just like you

LESLIE MEANS
HER VIEW FROM HOME

TYNDALE
MOMENTUM®

A Tyndale nonfiction imprint

Visit Tyndale online at tyndale.com.

Visit Tyndale Momentum online at tyndalemomentum.com.

Visit the author at https://herviewfromhome.com.

Tyndale, Tyndale's quill logo, *Tyndale Momentum*, and the Tyndale Momentum logo are registered trademarks of Tyndale House Ministries. Tyndale Momentum is a nonfiction imprint of Tyndale House Publishers, Carol Stream, Illinois.

So God Made a Mother: Tender, Proud, Strong, Faithful, Known, Beautiful, Worthy, and Unforgettable— Just Like You

So God Made a Mother is a trademark of *Her View From Home*, LLC

Designed by Dean H. Renninger

Published in association with Folio Literary Management, LLC, 630 9th Avenue, Suite 1101, New York, NY 10036.

For information about special discounts for bulk purchases, please contact Tyndale House Publishers at csresponse@tyndale.com, or call 1-855-277-9400.

Library of Congress Cataloging-in-Publication Data

A catalog record for this book is available from the Library of Congress.

ISBN 978-1-4964-6468-2 (Hardcover)

Printed in the United States of America

29   28   27   26   25   24   23
8   7   6   5   4

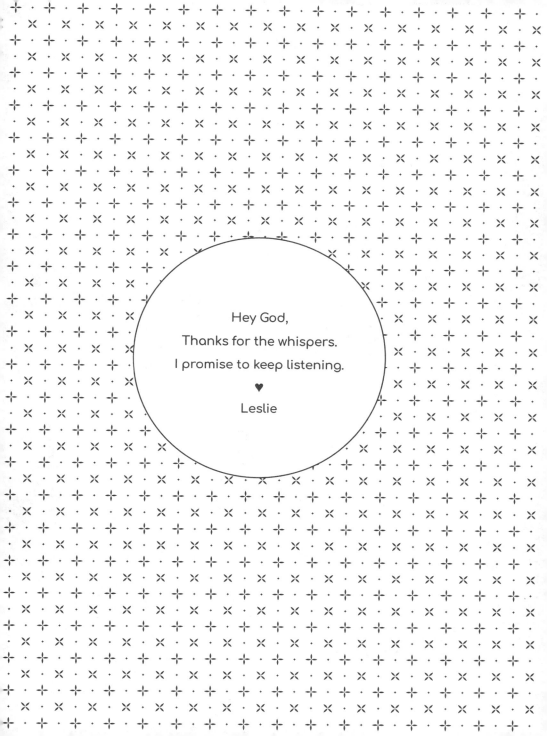

Hey God,

Thanks for the whispers.

I promise to keep listening.

♥

Leslie

Contents

✕

Foreword

Last night I sat on the floor in my pantry and ate half a bag of those miniature powdered donuts alone. Was it my finest hour? Probably not. But my entire family is sick. I've checked temperatures. I've made meals. I've rubbed backs. We've had doctor's appointments. I've kept everyone's medications organized and on schedule. The only faces I've seen for a solid week are the ones on TV and the ones I live with.

I've also done the whole "Is it my fault we're sick? Have we had enough vitamins? Am I doing a good enough job taking care of everyone?" thing. I've blamed myself. I've questioned myself. I've worried. Bless the good Lord, have I worried.

At one point yesterday, a little voice from the couch beckoned, "Mo-om!" and my shoulders instantly slumped. I closed my eyes, dropped my head down so my chin almost touched my chest, and breathed one long, slow inhale, mustering all the energy in my body to come alive and answer that call again.

Just then, a friend sent me a text. *Check your front porch. We moms have to stick together. Love ya, friend.*

Outside was a goody bag with all my favorite things: fresh flowers—lilies and hydrangeas and I don't even know what else, but they were bright and beautiful and so needed—chocolate, magazines, the sweetest handwritten card, and you guessed it, powdered donuts.

That act of love, it got me through.

Years ago, after my third baby was born, I found myself in a hole. I didn't recognize it at the time, but I wasn't just overwhelmed. I wasn't just tired. I wasn't just angry and lonely and sad. I was depressed. A mom friend with kids around the same age as mine recognized my struggle and took me out to dinner. Over chips and salsa, I opened up for the first time in a long time, with no shame, and finally found the courage to get some help.

And that act of love, it got me through.

I've witnessed so many acts of love between moms. The porch drop-offs. The encouraging notes. The little nods of solidarity as we pass each other in the grocery store. The invitations. The conversations at the park. The check-ins. And it all gets us through.

Someone saying, "I see you" gets us through. Little lifelines of hope get us through.

It's why I love Leslie and the *Her View From Home* community so much. Leslie knows how to create connections that have ripple effects, simply as women share their stories.

I think it's because our stories remind us we're not alone, even when we feel like we are. When we dig deep, get vulnerable, and say, "This is where I am. This is what I've been facing. This is what I've learned—maybe it will help you, too," we find camaraderie. We find comfort. We find peace. We find joy. We find grace. We find freedom. We find each other. We find ourselves.

I think you'll be able to pick this book up at any stage of your life and find little pieces of yourself in it, and that's a powerful thing. These stories, they hold us close. They point us in the right direction. They whisper peace. They give us hope. They ground us. They steady us. They lead us home.

These acts of love we share with and for each other, they bind us. We do it for each other. We do it for the next generation. We do it because somewhere along the way, someone dropped donuts on our doorstep when we were in the midst of a storm, and it got us through.

And what a privilege it is—what an absolute honor to reach out to another soul and help them through.

Amy Weatherly
Coauthor of the national bestseller I'll Be There (But I'll Be Wearing Sweatpants)

Introduction

LESLIE MEANS

✕

When I was a girl, my dad read bedtime stories to my sister and me. The books varied over the years, but one thing was constant: Dad never missed a night. At least, not in my memory.

When I was little, the stories were easy and often came from a Little Golden Book my three older sisters had read before me. The pages were usually tattered or riddled with graffiti—a side effect of hand-me-down books.

Eventually Dad started reading longer, more complicated titles, and then my sister and I started reading to him. He fell asleep sometimes, which always made us laugh.

One night his poker buddies arrived early, before Dad had a chance to read to us. I don't know if they started without him or if they just waited patiently in our kitchen. (Snacks probably helped the wait.) But I do know it didn't bother my dad. He didn't rush the process—he didn't skip a page or cut our reading time short. He made it clear that his priorities were his girls.

I'm not sure when we stopped our evening book-reading routine. I'd imagine it was around junior high, when I was too cool to associate with my parents. But I do know I'll never forget it.

What I've learned in my forty years of life is that those moments with my dad weren't about the stories in the books. Those moments helped me feel and know love. Unconditional love. The kind of love that helps a kid grow into a decent adult.

The kind of love that inspired me to get this book into your hands.

Mom had a huge part in this too, of course.

We didn't have money. We certainly didn't have clout. But we had love. We knew love.

And I know I'm giving that same love to my kids. At least, I'm trying.

And friend, I know you're trying too.

When you're changing diapers and cutting chicken nuggets into three hundred pieces and driving tweens and teens all over town (seriously, at some point we just become taxi drivers), it's hard to believe what you're doing is valuable.

You might start listening to the lie that makes you wonder if you're worthy of this gig. The lie tells you you're doing it wrong. You're messing up your kids. You're just a normal girl, doing normal things, with no real accolades to your name. The lie makes you wonder if this is all there is.

I know because I believed that lie too.

But at night, when the house is dark and the kids are in bed and the cat is asleep and my husband, Kyle, is snoring beside me (how does that man fall asleep in thirty seconds when it takes me an hour?), I hear God's whispers:

You are so loved.

What you're doing is important.

Your story is extraordinary.

Extraordinary? Really, God? I'm just an average girl in middle America. I once placed a clothespin on my nose, hoping it would make it smaller, and I nearly failed tenth-grade math. Trust me—I'm not that great.

God and I have interesting conversations.

But then I imagine Him giving me a look—the look Mom and Dad gave me when they didn't like what I was doing. The same look I now give my kids. The you-know-better-than-that look.

And somewhere along the way, I realized I'm supposed to let you know that you know better too, friend.

It's why I started the website *Her View From Home* more than a decade ago. I had no money or business experience, but I had God's whispers and a fire in my soul.

I knew the world needed a place where women could tell their extraordinary stories. Today, thousands of writers and millions of views later, *Her View From Home* is a community where women across the globe write about motherhood, marriage, relationships, grief, and faith with breathtaking vulnerability.

Now those writers are sharing their stories with you in this collection of real, honest, heartfelt stories. I pray you'll find comfort, laughter, peace, friendship, love, faith, and community in the words on these pages and the stories flowing from these hearts.

Maybe you'll even find your own story.

And if you do—*when* you do—I hope you know this gig you've been called to has always been worthy, valuable, and important. Not because you earned a fancy degree or won an award. Not because of the size of your bank account or the size of your jeans (or nose). But because you love your kids and you love your family and you are loved by God.

So God made a mother. And He made you extraordinary.

PART 1

SO GOD MADE A MOTHER

tender

✕

He needed someone with a heart tender enough to rock babies in the still, small hours of the night but strong enough to let them spread their wings and fly... so God made a MOTHER.

HER VIEW FROM HOME

The Shed

LESLIE MEANS

I can't remember when I first noticed it. It was probably sometime in the fall of 2008, when my newborn and I would drive (and drive and drive) to ease her crying and my nerves.

We'd pop in a Bon Jovi CD (remember those?) and hit the road until the tears stopped—hers and mine.

We spent hours together on those open roads. I often took gravel routes, hoping the hum of the car would soothe her to sleep.

On one of our adventures, I saw it. A sleepy shed at the edge of a cornfield, right along my favorite country road.

To some, this shed probably looked like the perfect setting for a scene out of a horror film. Especially right before harvest, when the corn was devouring it.

But I loved it.

Eventually I changed my route to my kids' daycare, just so I could drive by that cornfield and that shed.

Year after year, I watched it change. It grew and stretched and buckled under the weight of snow and rain and the harsh Midwest weather.

I grew and stretched too. Right when I thought our daycare years were over, my husband and I found out we were expecting our third child. A little boy.

Which meant I had at least five more years to drive by that shed.

Then one day, while on my normal route with our youngest, I noticed that the shed had changed. The shingles were worn. Its roof had started to cave.

I sobbed.

Right there in my car, on that familiar road, with my soon-to-be five-year-old strapped in his seat behind me, the tears fell.

I knew, as all moms know, this route, this road, this baby—would soon be gone.

The shed would crumble.

The gravel road would be paved.

And that baby? He'd start school in the fall. There would be no more reason to drive that route or visit that shed or take him to daycare.

A path I'd known for thirteen years would become a memory. That's motherhood, I suppose. The bittersweet journey of saying goodbye.

Mothers feel that ache deep in our souls, in that soft, mushy part of our hearts we try so hard to protect. But that tenderness? That ache? It's really just love, and it makes the road worth traveling, even when it brings us to tears.

You'll see that tenderness in these next several stories, I think—and you'll realize you're not the only one whose heart feels exposed as you love and launch your babies.

I'll Love
Every Version
of You

KRISTA WARD

Every time I look at you, I can't help but see so many versions of you.

The you you once were, when I held you in my arms for the first time. As you smiled that first smile, took your first steps.

The you who mispronounced words and fell asleep in your car seat, your limp body snuggled against mine as I carried you to bed.

The you who learned to ride a bike, beaming with pride as you sailed down the uneven sidewalk, shouting, "Look, Mommy! I'm doing it!"

The you who would grab for my hand as we'd stroll to the park after dinner. The you who wore pajamas and rain boots as you waltzed up and down the aisles of the grocery store.

All the versions after that as you grew and changed and transformed before my eyes, faster than my heart ever could have been prepared for.

And oh, how my heart aches.

Because that little you—I miss that you sometimes.

Other times when I look at you, I see you years from now.

There's a look in your eye, or maybe it's something in your sweet smile, and all of a sudden I see the you you'll become.

A glimpse of your future. *Our* future.

And oh, how my heart aches.

Because that you—I can't wait to love that version of you too.

But as I soak in every precious, intricate detail of the you before me, I've decided I'll simply love you right now.

The you who you are in this exact moment. Wonderful, incredible, uniquely you.

Because though I've loved all the versions of you before and I'll love all the versions of you to come, right now is a fleeting, irreplaceable gift.

So tonight, as I allow every bit of you to imprint on my heart, I won't see the you of yesterday. I won't see the you of tomorrow. I'll love you right now.

Krista Ward, creator of *Kisses from Boys*, is a wife and mom with a heart for encouraging others through every messy, beautiful moment of motherhood.

I Wait Outside My Teenager's Bedroom Door

WHITNEY FLEMING

I hear my daughter's door softly click shut from three rooms away as I stand at the kitchen sink. The mental image of an impenetrable bank vault creaking closed pops into my mind.

She arrives home just after 8 p.m., walking into our house looking tired but happy. My teenager spent her day going to high school, then sports practice, then a team dinner. I haven't seen her since 6:30 a.m.

She gives me a quick hello, then says she needs to take a shower and finish some homework.

"I'm going up to my room," she says over her shoulder, carrying an oversized bookbag packed to the gills.

Then I hear her door click shut.

Sometimes I hate the sound that door makes. It's a constant three-inch-wide reminder that my teenager would often rather be where I am not.

Where I can't ask questions.

Where I can't reach out to hug her.

Where I can't offer a solution to whatever problem she's facing.

Where I can't enjoy her presence and she doesn't have to endure mine.

The shift between us was subtle. She started doing her homework in her room instead of at the kitchen table. "So I can focus, Mom," she explained.

She would casually say she wanted to video chat a friend, then disappear for hours. I could hear her laughter through the walls, the murmur of her favorite music slipping through the cracks.

She would come home from school or practice or a social outing and, after giving me an obligatory greeting and grunt, head to her room, where I would hear the click of her door shutting me out of her world. Again.

I know this is the way it's supposed to happen—her quest for independence, for privacy, for growing up.

But even though she sits a mere one hundred feet away, the gulf between us is vast. And I miss her.

She is not an unruly child. She does well in school, she is kind and responsible, and she even puts her cups in the dishwasher most of the time. It's not that I don't trust what she's doing behind closed doors—I just want access to her.

Our relationship has changed. Where I used to be the center of her universe, I now find myself more of a spectator, often watching from a distance, waiting to be invited into her world. I am on the outside, wishing she would tell me how her day went, waiting for her to open her bedroom door and let me in for a moment.

I often don't know how to handle the emotions of watching my baby grow up, this juxtaposition of pride as I see the person she is becoming and grief as I remember the child she was. Her desire to break free is strong, and the fracture hurts me more. It's a dance we are both trying to lead.

Sometimes figuring out how to navigate this new terrain is challenging. *Don't ask too many questions. Don't comment about too many things. Don't give too much advice. Don't breathe too loudly. Definitely don't try to come through the bedroom door.*

So while she sequesters herself in the sanctuary of her room, I do the only thing I can—the only thing I can control: I make myself more available than ever before.

I fold laundry and pay bills at the kitchen counter on the off chance she will come down for a snack.

I offer to give rides and buy frozen yogurt when I am bone-tired after a long day of work.

I keep my bedroom door wide open in the hope she will need to borrow tweezers or black socks or a pair of earrings for a class presentation the next day.

And in those rare moments when she emerges, I am there for whatever small part of her life she will share with me.

It is different, this new paradigm. Our relationship is more on her terms than on mine, and I must be okay with that.

I listen more, I nod, I hold back on giving advice. I try to be patient, I try to be understanding, I try to remember what it was like to want to break free from my parents so badly it hurt. I try to remember what it was like to be a teenager who hid behind her bedroom door.

This new stage of parenting is an evolution in my relationship with her. It is a revolution for my daughter.

And as we continue to forge this new terrain, I am desperate for our relationship to come out stronger on the other side.

So, as painful as it is, I let her stay behind that bedroom door as much as she needs to. I let her go to hold on. I let her go, knowing one day we will find common ground again. I let her go, knowing breaking free does not mean breaking up. I let her go, knowing one day she will come back to me.

I still hate the sound of that door closing, but I love what's behind it so much more.

Whitney Fleming co-runs the blog *Parenting Teens & Tweens* and posts her musings about life at *Whitney Fleming Writes* on Facebook and Instagram.

The Bittersweet Last Baby

CASEY HUFF

A few weeks ago, our nearly three-year-old daughter started asking me to rock her to sleep in the recliner next to the fireplace. We sit there, she snuggled under a blanket and I wrapped around her, feeling her weight in my arms and smelling traces of lavender shampoo in her hair.

Back and forth, back and forth we sway as she yawns and fights heavy eyelids.

Sometimes she tells me sleepily about the horse she saw out the car window earlier that day or the funny thing that happened at Nana's house. Other times she's so tired she falls asleep in three seconds flat, and I'm left to listen to the hum of her little snores and stare at her delicate features.

When I look at her in the dim light of the fire's glow, it's hard not to see her as she was when she was only a few weeks old and we did this same dance. Back and forth, back and forth in this worn, gray chair.

I catch myself staring with the same awe and intensity as when we first brought her home from the hospital. Memorizing her features. Admiring her long, thick lashes. Feeling my heart swell with adoration and pride. Pushing down the lump in my throat when I think about how much I wish she would stay this age for just a little while longer.

I've been tucking these nightly moments into my heart, because I know they'll quickly become a thing of the past.

This precious little girl of mine—she's the last. Our baby, even though she's no longer much of a baby at all. The finality of that makes my heart ache sometimes.

After her, I will have no more little ones to rock—just big kids doing big things.

Raising her is a long series of goodbyes for our family. Goodbye to the newborn coos. The first smiles. The wobbly steps. The first birthdays. We're saying goodbye to all the seasons we've become so acquainted with since her oldest brother was born more than six years ago and our second son after that.

We've been so deep in the baby and toddler stages that sometimes it seemed like they would never end. But they will. They are.

If you've raised a last baby, you know just what I mean.

You have a unique perspective with your last that you don't have—can't possibly have—with your first. You know some chapters really do end.

You watch as they outgrow their little footie pajamas and their sippy cups and your arms.

You cheer as they take their first steps, only to realize when you lay your head on your pillow that they were the final wobbly steps one of your babies will take across your kitchen floor.

You're desperate for them to sleep through the night, but when they do, you long for the quiet midnight meetings shared between just the two of you.

You eagerly mark their first birthdays on the calendar, but after the candle has been blown out, it dawns on you that your last first year is over.

You've been through each of these transitions with your other kids, it's true. But somehow when you have more babies coming up behind them, the lasts don't seem like such a big deal. You'll still have diapers to change, outlet covers to replace, and bottles to warm.

But when it's your last baby—when your family is complete and tied up with a little pink or blue bow—every milestone marks the closing of a chapter. Not just for your baby, but for you too.

As time goes on, you'll find yourself falling into more and more of the clichés about parenting a youngest child. The stereotypes will echo in your head when you let more things slide or throw out the rulebook. Or when you agree to rock her to sleep every night instead of insisting she's old enough to fall asleep on her own.

It's then you'll know the truth: it's not that parents set out to spoil the last baby—it's that they're desperately grasping for the precious season they see dissolving before their eyes, one they're not quite ready to let go of.

Watching your last baby grow up is like breaking off pieces of your heart to store away in a vault. You can revisit the memories whenever you want, but it will never be the same as experiencing them in real time.

Your last baby will change you forever.

They'll bring you joy.

Make you a little more sentimental.

Leave you second-guessing if they are, in fact, really meant to be your last.

They'll show you you're capable of a love vaster than you ever imagine and that hearts really can grow infinite sizes.

Your last will make you hold them close and never, ever want to let go.

So no matter how tired I am—no matter how many dishes are in the sink or how many piles of laundry are on the bed or how many to-dos have yet to be done—I'll say yes to every date with my daughter in that old, well-loved rocking chair.

She's our last baby, and it's the greatest honor of my life to hold her like this for as long as she'll let me.

Casey Huff is mom to three amazing kids and wife to a great guy. She writes to help other women find solidarity in their motherhood journey.

You Don't Have to Live like You're Dying

MANDY McCARTY HARRIS

✕

Somehow we've taken to heart the idea that we need to live like we're dying.

Not only are we supposed to do all the things required to stay alive, but we're supposed to do them while making the most of every single moment. *Go, go, go! Make those memories! Go big or go home! It's a good day to have a good day! Those memories aren't going to make themselves!*

That's more pressure than any of us can live up to. If I had to guess, most of us have missed out on more than a few precious moments because we were too busy trying to make them count to notice whether they did or not.

But we're missing the mark when we try to live every day with such urgency. I would know.

Our daughters were diagnosed with an aggressive neurodegenerative disease when they were four and six years old. How long did they have? So many factors could come into play, but barring a miracle or massive scientific breakthrough, our daughters wouldn't live to adulthood. Any way you sliced it, the truth was in front of us: our girls were dying.

Our initial reaction was exactly as you'd expect. We had to hurry up and live! There was no time to waste! So we set out to live like we were dying.

There were many sparkly moments with our girls over the next few years, but the majority of our days were spent in the slow, ordinary, uneventful moments of life.

Our daughters died when they were seven and eleven years old, and my most treasured memories of them weren't the result of our urgency to chase big, flashy experiences. My most precious times with them were ordinary moments—so wonderfully and beautifully ordinary.

Evening reading and bedtime prayers were gifts of simple goodness. We didn't do these things as a family because our daughters had little time left. Bedtime routines remained the same because they were intimately ours. In those moments, we were quietly, safely, and gratefully together.

On Sunday mornings we joined our church family, and the girls hummed along with the choir in praise. We didn't go to church because our children were dying. We went to church because we love Jesus.

When they needed extra comfort, my girls would snuggle into me just as they did when they were babies. Our hearts beat together, and I breathed them in. I didn't orchestrate those moments because my girls had a terminal disease. Our bodies fit together because that's what God created them to do, and that remained true throughout their lives.

We *lived*. It wasn't flashy or momentous. We lived with and for our daughters, and the moments that are tattooed on my heart didn't come with fanfare.

Together, we chose what was most important to us, and then we snuggled up and drew close to one another. We set a necessary pace and rested when we needed to. We made time for silliness, laughter, and family traditions. But mostly, we were just together.

So lay down the urgency to make every day the best day ever. The treasures of life are found in ordinary moments, with the people you love, and you don't have to rush that.

Don't miss the mark by aiming only for the high points. Your life isn't an action movie, and you don't have to live like you're dying. All you have to do is show up and love your people. I promise that someday, when you or someone you love is nearing the end of this earthly life, you won't think back on the extravagant trips, the fancy parties, or the flashy moments. Instead, you'll close your eyes and breathe in the memories of ordinary moments when you were simply together.

And that will be enough.

Mandy McCarty Harris writes about grief, joy, faith, and real life on her blog, *Happy Like This*.

I Want My Kids to See the Good

AMY WEATHERLY

✕

I want to shield my kids from everything.

I want to shield them from evil and corruption and the news. I want to shield them from the fact that bad things happen, even to good people, and that sometimes there's no real reason for it.

I want to shield them from other kids who tell them they aren't fast enough or smart enough or good enough. I want to shield them from criticism. I want to shield them from harshness. I want to shield them from violence.

I don't want to tell them bad people exist. I don't want to tell them bad governments exist.

I don't want to tell them about wars and trials and hurricanes. I don't want to tell them about cancer. I don't want to tell them sometimes kids go hungry. I don't want to tell them sometimes people hate, for no real reason at all.

I want to shield my kids from every single fiery arrow this world is going to hurl in their direction.

I can shield them from some of it, but the truth is, a few of those arrows are going to land, no matter how I try to outmaneuver, outsmart, and outperform them. I worry about it all day, every day. I stress about their innocence being stripped away when I'm not looking. My mind is going every minute: *How do I protect them from [fill in the blank]? What do I do if [fill in the blank] happens?*

It's hard to be a mom. Anyone who says otherwise is a total liar. It's hard, and it's exhausting. The physical stuff, sure, but it's the mental load that will wear on you. Nobody prepared me for that part.

I'll always worry. I don't know how not to. And I'll always try to shield them and save as much of their innocence as possible, but the truth is, life is going to hit them in one way or another.

Some kid at school is going to run their mouth and tell them something I didn't want them to know quite yet, and I'll be forced into a conversation neither of us was prepared for.

Some bully on the playground is going to chip away at their confidence, one insult at a time. They'll learn about wars. They'll learn people argue about non-sense on social media and that sometimes things are polarized and divided even though they shouldn't be. They'll learn not everyone has a good heart.

A friend will leave them out. They'll probably have a teacher who doesn't like them, and they'll feel the animosity. They'll get rejected. They'll get knocked down. They'll learn that Santa isn't real and that fairytales aren't true and that this world is an imperfect place, full of imperfect people.

So yes, shield your kids from everything you possibly can. Protect their child-hood. But make sure you also point out whenever you see kindness happening between two strangers. Bake chocolate chip cookies, cover them with aluminum foil, and take them to neighbors you haven't met yet on a random Tuesday after-noon and tell them this is how we love each other.

Take them on walks in the woods and stare in wonder at the size of a tree trunk or the beauty of a wildflower. Marvel at the way a caterpillar turns into a butterfly. Get down on the ground so they can feel the grass in between their toes, and let them play in the mud.

Teach them to be good to their friends—like really, really good. And tell them what a gift it is to have people in their lives who love them and see them and show up for them.

Let them hear music and paint and delight in creativity.

Take them outside and let them fall in love with the stars and the hugeness of the sky. Teach them about fish and birds and ecosystems and the way this wild world somehow keeps spinning on God's powerful fingertip. Teach them this entire earth and everything in it exists because we are the exact right distance from the sun and because we're tilted to the exact right degree.

When tragedy strikes and a tornado ravages a town, let them see how people come from near and far to donate their own blood to help people they'll never meet.

Laugh. Laugh a whole lot. Laugh every chance you get. Help and give and apologize. Love other people, and love them in really big ways, because your kids are going to find out soon enough that things aren't perfect.

No matter how you try to shield them, they'll eventually see this world is messy and chaotic and hard. But if you do it right, and if you're intentional about it, they'll see this world is beautiful too.

They'll see more people are good than bad, and they'll see each one of us—even people living a million miles away—has a part to play.

They'll marvel at our Creator's handiwork. They'll have hope for the future and a sense of purpose today.

They'll look at life as the miracle it is, flaws and all. They'll see the way these jagged puzzle pieces eventually fit together. And they'll know that life may be hard, but God is great.

Amy Weatherly is a wife and a mom of three. She's coauthor of the national bestseller *I'll Be There (But I'll Be Wearing Sweatpants)*.

Our Rainbow Baby Healed My Broken Heart

STACEY SKRYSAK

×

My heart raced and my jaw clenched as I looked around the hospital room, a place filled with so many memories from that fateful day six years earlier. As the nurses hooked up monitors, my tears began to fall. I was about to give birth to our rainbow baby in the very same hospital where two of my triplets passed away.

Pregnancy did not come easily for me. Years of infertility led to in vitro fertilization and, eventually, the shock of our lives: my husband and I were expecting triplets—two identical girls and a boy. And even though my pregnancy was high risk, I basked in the glow of nurturing three babies in my womb.

But life didn't go as planned. The picture-perfect family we imagined turned to heartbreak after I went into labor at twenty-two weeks gestation. Peyton, Parker, and Abigail were born more than seventeen weeks premature. Their tiny bodies weighed just over one pound each. Their eyes were fused shut, and their skin was translucent. Doctors tried to save our firstborn child, but Abigail's lungs were just too weak. She passed away in our arms about two hours after birth.

Our remaining triplets were whisked off to the neonatal intensive care unit. As days turned into weeks, we grieved the loss of one child while trying to remain strong for our other two.

But two months later, our hearts shattered again when our son became gravely ill. At fifty-five days old, Parker passed away in our arms. Two of my children died in a matter of months, initiating me to a club no parent ever wants to be part of.

I found myself in a balancing act, finding ways to celebrate our surviving triplet while wondering what life would be like if her siblings had survived. We considered trying for more children, but deep down I was scared to have another baby. The fear of pregnancy and loss was too much for my heart to handle.

But God had other plans for our family. Exactly six years after we started fertility treatments, I stared at the two pink lines of a positive pregnancy test. As a shocked smile washed over my husband's face, I was overcome with emotion. I realized I had to face my fears head on.

Rainbow baby is a term used to describe a child born after loss. Some say the baby offers families hope, a rainbow at the end of a storm. But ask any parent who has endured this tragedy: even though there is new life, it doesn't mean it's filled with rainbows and happiness.

You never get over the loss of a child. You never forget. A piece of your heart will always ache for the child you can't hold in your arms. The constant worry that this baby might not survive is mingled with anxiety and grief. While the world may think you're getting a happy ending, your heart hurts, because no baby can ever replace your child who died.

As I lay in that hospital bed, familiar faces filled the room; the same nurses and doctors who delivered my triplets all those years before were there. Almost six years to the day after my son passed away in the same hospital, I gave birth to a healthy baby girl. Life had come full circle.

Doctors placed our newborn on my chest, and her tiny, warm body nuzzled into my skin, her strong heartbeat a reminder that this moment was its own. Reality set in as I began to sob—we would leave the hospital with a healthy baby in our arms this time.

My tears that day were bittersweet, filled with memories of the past and hope for our future. Because while the loss of a child changes you forever, a rainbow baby has a unique way of healing the heart.

Stacey Skrysak is a TV journalist and writer, specializing in child loss and premature birth. She is mom to a twenty-two-weeker surviving triplet and a rainbow baby.

I'm Still Learning to Let Go

LISA WAECHTER-CASS

I vividly remember each time my husband and I brought our children home from the hospital as newborns. Our hours were filled with laughter, smiles, dirty diapers, balancing work, and late-night feedings, yet I never considered how I would someday have to learn to let it all go.

Don't get me wrong—I was happy to let go of the dirty diapers, daycare bills, and sleepless nights. There's no glamour or fame during midnight blowouts or the times you show up to work wearing spit-up on your shirt. But during those early days, my babies were all under my roof, tucked in their comfortable beds. Safe. When we were raising those babies, it was hard to imagine them as adults. That day seemed to be so far in the future that I put it in the back of my mind.

Twenty-three years later, we are parents to two adult children, a teenager, and a preteen. My children have taught me so much about letting go.

A major catalyst in helping me understand the importance of letting go—and having deeper faith—was our son Gabe, who died of hypoplastic left heart syndrome after only eleven hours of life.

God's timing is always perfect, even when we don't understand the lessons in the moment. Letting go is a process that takes time.

I love this quote from Eleanor Brownn: "Letting go may sound so simple, but rarely is it a one-time thing. Just keep letting go, until one day it's gone for good." From the moment we meet our children, they are not ours to keep. Gabe taught me this. We are the guardians of our children, but ultimately their paths in life are their own.

We have always had high expectations of our children, but the most important expectation is that they are safe and successful on their own terms. I don't mourn the loss of having them live in my basement—I mean, I like having my office back. But I do miss the day-to-day conversations, hearing about their lives and talking to their friends. And to be truthful, it's taken me a while to get used to not having to cook for six people in this house.

My kids are so much of who I have been. Maybe in this process of letting go, I am mourning who I used to be too. I won't be here forever, and my hope is that they will be there for each other when their dad and I are long gone.

To all the new and experienced mamas out there: don't lose yourself in the process of raising your children. Save a little energy for yourself. Accept God's forgiveness when you mess up. Every. Single. Time. And, despite what well-meaning friends and family may say, allow yourself to grieve during this process of letting go.

It's okay to feel sad when kids go to college or to a foreign country, but don't stay in that sadness too long. Do something for yourself. Eat healthy, take a walk, listen to music, visit old friends. The goal is to raise independent children who will grow up and become contributing members of society.

It's okay to feel sad that you no longer have the ability to protect them from every tough life lesson they'll encounter in this big, scary world. But if we've done our job well—and I hope I have—our adult kids will let us know when they need our guidance and support.

The process of loving and letting go of grown children is bittersweet. I may cry, but they are tears of joy, because I am so incredibly grateful God made me their mama.

Lisa Waechter-Cass grew up in the land of Willa Cather. She is a wife, mother, and educator who loves her family and friends dearly.

The Ache

MIKALA ALBERTSON

Going in, I knew it would end. I just never anticipated The Ache.

From the first moment I startled awake into motherhood, I felt thrilled. Panicked. Full of delight. And filled with the tiniest bit of dread. I could see myself from above—teary eyed, mesmerized by the sight of my beautiful baby, and fully understanding in one perfect, holy instant: this ends.

And so, The Ache began even as I caught a glimpse of what hadn't even begun.

From the very beginning, I hoped that love would be strong enough to hold.

As I pulled my pink, squalling newborn to my bare chest, I silently prayed. *Love, love, love, love, love.*

He learned to roll and crawl and walk. I chased him as he ran on pudgy toddler legs, and I listened to him squeal in a bubbly bath. He started out with "Mama," then quickly learned to talk, and I remembered to write down all his silly made-up words. He moved from crib to toddler bed with bright red and blue cars printed on the sheets.

And each night as I snuggled next to him in the dark before he fell asleep, I silently prayed. *Love, love, love, love, love.*

I taught him how to ride a bike. I sang the "Happy Birthday" song year after year. His nose became dotted with freckles. And sometimes when he wrapped his wiry little arms around my waist for a tight squeeze, I tried to memorize those giant Chiclet teeth decorating his bright smile. *Love, love, love, love, love.*

There were so many qualities I attempted to impress on my boy over the years. I hoped he would learn about kindness and compassion. I tried to instill a bit of work ethic and perseverance. I wanted him to learn empathy. Integrity. A beautiful, unwavering faith.

I worried that sometimes I came across as controlling. Maybe a little annoyed or frustrated. Disappointed, even. As his mother, I've certainly messed up in a million ways.

But each night as he leaned in for a limp-armed hug and maybe even an eye roll, I silently prayed. *Love, love, love, love, love.*

I watch him a bit wistfully these days. While dinner simmers on the stove, I find myself leaning against the doorway in the kitchen in that place we mark the kids' heights along the wall. Sometimes I call out, "Careful, you guys," while he and his brother have a wrestling match in the living room. I say it in a half-hearted voice, because I don't really want them to stop.

These wrestling matches and his favorite meal of enchiladas on the stove mean a little more to me lately. Because of The Ache.

But I'm noticing the ways he is kind and compassionate. The challenges he faced in the past year gave me a glimpse into his work ethic. And I'm incredibly proud of his integrity and grace.

Love did that. Not mine, but His. And I'm left to soak it all in.

Yes, The Ache reminds me regularly that this ends. But now I understand, with all my heart, love holds. *Love, love, love, love, love.*

Pressed down, shaken together, running over. Love is strong enough to hold.

Mikala Albertson is a wife, mother of five, part-time family doctor, and author of *Ordinary on Purpose: Surrendering Perfect and Discovering Beauty Amid the Rubble.*

We're Holding On to Love

AMY BETTERS-MIDTVEDT

✕

"You know, Mom, things have finally gotten better between us, and I think I know why."

I stopped what I was doing and glanced at my girl, all grown up and beautiful and offering me her honest thoughts.

I stopped, anxious to hear her words but afraid of what she was going to say. You see, ours has not been an easy road lately.

Over the last few years, I've spent hours thinking about how I must have flat-out done everything wrong. And then there were moments I thought I had clearly done everything right and yet my child was doing everything wrong, and it was baffling. I cried and raged and worried and wondered how on earth it was all going to end. I worried the answer was *in complete disaster*.

Those moments of despair usually came when she didn't show up at home for dinner or at curfew, or when she wouldn't come out of her room, or when she was slamming all the doors, or when we found questionable objects in her bedroom or in her purse, or when, despite her amazing grades and wonderful friends, all we could see were the ways everything was falling apart under the shiny surface.

All the things we swear our sweet innocent babies will never do when they are teenagers? She was making her way right down the list. I was left asking how my well-loved and amazing kid could be running full force from the rules we set and from every bit of advice we gave. So we made more rules and gave more advice. What could possibly be wrong with that?

I have never prayed so hard as I did for God to watch out for this child. I reminded myself over and over that He loved her even more than I did. But couldn't He see fit to steer her back toward at least the middle of the road instead of letting her veer straight off it?

The summer before she left for college, I hung on by a thread, both wishing she weren't leaving but also looking forward to the peace that would come when every single day wouldn't be so darn hard. I'm not sure who felt it more, actually—her or me.

When she left, we sort of took a breath, although much of what I worried about just followed her there. It turned out worrying and wondering from a distance wasn't always easier, and the knot in my stomach decided to stay right where it was.

Then all at once, her classes went online and she returned to her childhood bedroom.

I cried in the shower, and I'm ashamed to say I was crying for me. My break was over. I was heading back to constant, in-my-face worrying and the brutality of watching the girl who once wouldn't let me leave the house without giving me a series of very specific kisses and hugs look at me like she wished she were anywhere but near me.

But we had no choice except to figure it out.

And somehow, under the same roof again, we found our way back to each other.

It turns out I had been given the gift of fresh eyes, created by distance and hope and the love that had always burned for her in my heart. That perspective enabled me to see the beauty of my girl again as she made her way out of her room and back to us. All I had to do was lift the curtain of fear that had hidden her from me for so long.

I wanted so badly for her to be well and happy that I'd been blind to the miracle she already was. I'd been so focused on the mistakes and missteps that I'd forgotten she and I were already both enough, right there in our brokenness.

I could finally see how my fear was hurting her—how instead of keeping her safe, it made me an unsafe person for her to come to. The fear I was holding on to was driving us apart.

So I decided to put aside fear and pick up love. And loving her meant letting her be free. Free to let her mistakes be hers and mine be mine. Free to learn her own lessons, even when it was the absolute hardest way (why does it have to be the hardest way?). Free to pull herself up when she had to. Free to gain strength and confidence by forging her own path—something that wouldn't have happened if she'd just listened to me and done as she was told.

Once she was free to test her own wings, I was also free to help her get up and try again. And she felt it too.

"We are so much better, Mom. I think it's because you've finally learned to let go a bit more."

I held my breath.

"And I think I've finally learned it's okay to hold on."

Yes. The more she'd tried to pull away, the harder I held on. And the harder I held on, the harder she tried to pull away, until our tugs in opposite directions almost ripped each of us in two.

When I loosened my grip and she tightened hers, we were bound together in a way even deeper than when I'd held her in my arms after she first arrived on this earth. And our love held us fast.

Amy Betters-Midtvedt is a mom of five, wife, and educator. She shares her chaos and faith at *Hiding in the Closet with Coffee*.

My Mother's Gone, but I Still Need Her

MANDE SAITTA

✕

The day I flew home to Omaha in late August, I was a twisted knot of shock and anxiety, fear and heartbreak.

The call had come just twelve hours earlier, from my sister. Her voice caught at my greeting. "Mom had a heart attack," she said through tightly held tears.

I was on vacation with my family, and I booked the earliest flight I could. As I settled into my seat, I ran through the scenario I would likely encounter when seeing my mother in the ICU: the sterile hospital walls. The mishmash of wires and tubes. The beeps of monitors. The smell of bleach. The eyes of medical staff, peeking over N95 masks.

On the descent into Omaha, the pilot glided the plane through the bright blue sky toward my hometown. I watched the grid of land come closer as we passed through the wispy clouds. And I knew in the innermost part of my being that I was flying home to plan my mother's funeral.

I pushed the thought away. I certainly didn't dare to say it out loud—not to myself or to the family members I was communicating with. We kept operating under the assumption that after a long haul of hospital stays and rehabilitation, my mom would emerge to an existence that might look different, but she'd be alive nonetheless.

Or so my head hoped. My mouth spoke hopeful prayers, but my heart knew better.

Her death resulted from a domino of medical emergencies we never saw coming. It was sudden, yanking the breath from our lungs in the same way the cardiac arrest—likely brought on by the heart attack—took hers. It felt violent and aggressive, like whiplash on our stunned and shattered hearts.

I had seen my mom healthy just four weeks before that jarring phone call. On a stormy Saturday evening in August, my daughters and I met with her and my sister to shop at our old haunt. We pushed carts up and down the aisles, finding treasures. My mother picked out a sweater in the prettiest shade of lavender. For the chilly fall weather, she said.

Afterward we went to a local restaurant and gabbed over dinner. When we parted, Mom broke into tears while hugging my oldest daughter, who was moving to a nearby town for college. We promised to make the short drive to see her on a Saturday in September and have lunch.

September brought death instead. My mother was just sixty-three years old—I had no inkling I would lose her so soon. She never got to wear that beautiful sweater.

But God knew. He knows the number of all our days. He knew my mom was gifted with 22,881 days. No more, no less.

My mother was flawed but wonderful. The relationship between mothers and daughters can be complicated like that. Sometimes we warred. Often we belly laughed. We shared a great deal in common. I see the threads of her life running through so many aspects of my own. I recognize shades of her in my daughters, in my sisters, in the way I see the world, and in the way I parent. I marvel at the way God authors in us the echoes that carry through generations.

She was a good mother. She loved me, and I knew it. She wanted me, and I knew it. It's a blessing not everyone receives.

Just as I expected, the hospital room was sterile and bleak. But it was a holy place too. In the stillness of those walls, I had the privilege of watching the legacy of her life make a gentle landing, just like the plane that brought me home to her. There, I had the chance to sit at my mother's bedside and whisper to her how well she had done.

It was the sweetest balm to my soul to tell her. On the day she died, I smiled at the cool, autumn air lacing the morning. It was her absolute favorite kind of day. The light breeze danced through my hair as I allowed a truth to sink deep into my heart: I was made to always need a mother, to always be parented. And I'll never come to the end of grieving that lack. The joy and pain of knowing and then losing my mother would always coexist.

I will always be a mama. And I'll always need a mama.

It's the journey of motherhood—the incomparable story of tender moments and beloved memories—and it's worth every mile.

Mande Saitta lives in Nebraska. Married to a good man and mother to two beautiful daughters, you can find her blog musings at *Handiwork of Grace.*

As You Grow, My Love Remains

GINGER HUGHES

It's hard to believe she's almost outgrown this precious space—a simple but beautiful bassinet I selected with such care more than ten years ago.

Her older sister was the first to sleep here, followed by her big brother three years later. After each of their births, it stood vigil beside our bed those first few months. I wanted to be certain to hear any sound, any movement, any indication my baby might need me.

It wasn't long before each baby outgrew that little bassinet and moved into a crib in their very own room. My heart lurched a bit when it was time to make the change; it happened so fast. So many nights I would lie on the floor, one arm reaching up through the slats of the crib, patting my little one's back and singing lullabies until sleep came.

One day turned into another, and just like that, the crib was stored away, replaced by a twin-size bed. I remember looking at my daughter, and later my son, appearing so small at first in that gargantuan bed, but that is no longer the case. Now each morning, long, lanky legs kick off covers as the kids make their way downstairs to greet the day.

Watching my children move from bassinet to crib to bed has taught me something over the years: motherhood is one long lesson in change, one continuous transition.

It's transitioning from breastfeeding or bottle-feeding to pureed baby foods, from finger foods to "Mama, may we have pizza on Friday night?"

It's storing the tiny infant tub that once held space on the kitchen counter to tub baths filled with toys to a locked bathroom door, ensuring no one interrupts a shower.

It's packing away onesies at record speed to be replaced by little polka-dot jumpers and socks with ruffles. The winds blow and the seasons change, and your daughter, who now stands almost as tall as you, shakes her head in perplexed disgust as you hold up what you believe to be a pretty cool outfit at the local department store. And we're left shaking our heads, wondering where the time has gone and how we got here so fast.

It's the daddy-daughter Valentine's dance, her dress floating as she twirls excitedly in front of the mirror. The next thing you know, you're shopping for just the right dress for the prom.

It's cheering until your voice is raspy at his first Little League game and then cheering from the stands for Friday-night football.

It's walking hand in hand through those big preschool doors, smiling brightly enough for both of you as your little one looks around with uncertainty. And it's walking away with tears in your eyes because you're still learning to let him go.

It's graduations and college orientation and "Mama, she said yes!" Yet something inside you feels as though he was just right beside you in tiny footed pajamas, sleeping snugly in this simple but beautiful bassinet.

And that's motherhood. It's a series of transitions and learning to navigate change. It's a lesson in letting go. It's realizing there are seasons for everything under heaven and knowing nothing stays the same. It's trying hard, adapting, and messing up. It's catching our breath, beaming with pride, and soaking our pillows with tears. It's laughter and joy—so much joy. It's being thankful for mercies that are new each day and starting over once more.

Before having children, I didn't fully realize how quickly things change, how time flows like a river whose current steadily makes its way. It's the same with our children: they make their way. And we help and watch and cheer them on, because while everything else changes, there's one thing that remains constant: love.

Today a baby girl is once again sleeping in this little bassinet purchased a decade ago. I didn't know that would be the case. But one thing I do know is how quickly this time will pass—how, in just a few weeks, we'll make the transition from the bassinet to the crib, and then one day not so long from now, to a twin bed all her own. She will continue to grow and change and make her way in the world.

My breath will catch and my heart will squeeze and tears will fall with the passing of each milestone. The sun will slip below the horizon, and a new day will dawn. The seasons will change, as will most everything else.

But my love will always, always remain.

Ginger Hughes, a wife and mother of three, writes to encourage women in motherhood, life, and faith. Find her on social media at *No Mama's Perfect*.

PART 2

SO GOD MADE A MOTHER

proud

✕

EVEN WHEN I'M EXHAUSTED.

EVEN WHEN I MISS HAVING TIME TO MYSELF.

EVEN WHEN MOTHERHOOD FEELS OVERWHELMING.

I'd choose this life all over again, because nothing brings me more joy than getting to be your mom.

HER VIEW FROM HOME

The No

LESLIE MEANS

✕

My daughter Ella was getting ready to try out for a local play. She's never been a nervous kid. She makes friends easily and loves to talk. Theater is a perfect fit for her personality.

She practiced for a few weeks, and on the big day she put on her holiday socks (it's her thing) and walked confidently into that theater.

Her dad took her and sent me text messages throughout the audition.

"Nailed it," he said when she sang her piece and danced a little dance and read a few lines.

I prayed the judges would feel the same.

The next day I got a text from a friend. "Hey, the cast is already posted. You might want to check it out."

I was 98 percent sure Ella's name was on that list. I pulled up the website and handed over the phone for my girl to look.

"Do you see your name?" I asked, pacing nervously, praying her name was there.

"I don't see it, Mom."

In that instant, my heart was crushed.

I wanted to hug her and tell her everything would be okay.

I wanted to explain that sometimes we fail, and it makes us better kids, better teens, and eventually, better adults.

I wanted to tell her we learn and grow from rejection.

I wanted to tell her how good she is, how worthy she is, how I would always be her number one fan.

I wanted to tell her this meant something bigger was waiting for her.

I wanted to tell the judges they'd made a mistake. That my kid is good. She's such a joy. How could they not see that?

I wanted to tell her she could give me all her pain and all her sorrow and all her fears and all her hurt. I would take it for her. I would pile it on my shoulders until the day I die.

I wanted to cry. This was one of my hardest moments as a mom. Harder than childbirth and late nights and endless crying and temper tantrums and fourth-grade math.

I wanted to tell her all of this. But I didn't have to.

"Mom," she said, "my friend made it! That's cool!"

And: "Wow, this cast isn't very big. I bet it was hard for the judges to decide."

And: "I wonder if they still need help backstage."

And: "I'll try again, Mom. It was fun!"

That crushed heart of mine? It became instantly proud. It turns out I was the one who needed to be reminded it's all okay.

That *no* makes our kids stronger.

That this won't weaken her heart—it will only help it grow.

That this was the first of many rejections she will receive throughout her life.

That my kid is going to make an incredible adult someday.

That I'm so proud to be her mom.

She'll try again. I will too.

Because that's what we do as mothers, right? Over and over, we grow right alongside the children we're raising. And sometimes they do it more effortlessly than we do.

Parenting a Wild Child Is Worth It All

JACQUELINE MILLER

×

It's after school, in the fast-food drive-thru line. We have fifteen minutes before my teen starts his shift at a shop nearby.

I spotted it first: a fire, with knee-high flames hopping up from the mulch. "Fire!"

"Yeah, right," my fifteen-year-old mumbled sarcastically, until his eyes locked on it too.

The weather had been dry lately. Really dry. My best guess is that someone flicked a still-lit cigarette on the ground, and the ground cover went up like kindling.

We were in the second lane, farthest from the burning flower bed. It didn't matter—my kid jumped out and ran . . . into the flames.

Parenting this child has always been a white-knuckle experience. Even before he was crawling, when he could only roll, he would hurl his tiny body toward electrical cords and try to chew on them. As soon as he could stand, he was hoisting his leg over the rails of his crib, trying to dive-bomb the carpet. He blew through every babyproofing effort like it was an obstacle set up for his amusement. He's been keeping us on our toes ever since.

So I wasn't surprised when I watched this boy in a man's body try to smother a fire outside a busy restaurant. He stomped and kicked the dirt, but it wasn't extinguishing as efficiently as I would have liked. When the flames threatened to lick his shins, I rolled down my window to yell something about aborting the mission, stat.

But he knew. This boy has better instincts than most. Before I could squeak out the first syllable, he was dashing toward the car to grab several bottles of water.

With everyone around us spectating, my long-legged teenager nonchalantly shouted over his shoulder as he (once again) ran toward the flames, "Ten-piece nuggets with BBQ, please."

He doused the blaze while white smoke billowed around him, then tamped it down for good measure.

When my teen climbed back into the car, reeking of his charred adventure, he declared that despite his efforts, the fire was still smoldering. Right on cue we watched it reignite, a fresh batch of flames aglow. At the same moment, a posse of employees arrived on the scene, armed with super-sized cups and eying a spigot not yet attached to a hose.

For his part, my son got his nuggets, devoured them in time for his shift, and continued on with his day. The event was barely a blip on his radar.

But for the rest of the night, I kept thinking, *My teenager just ran into a fire.*

No, I don't believe he was ever in any real danger. But he acted—immediately and without hesitation. My ninth grader was spurred into action while everyone else just sat there.

That really sums up our journey parenting a wild child who never fit the mold, who doesn't quite jibe with what the world expects of him. My son has learning differences that make his education a nonstop battle, but he can intuitively fix electronics or sense if someone's having a bad day. He thrives when operating a lathe or chopping wood or teaching little campers how to rig fishing lines. He favors a hammock under the stars, because who needs a bed or air-conditioning?

Last fall, when I bashed my ankle while on a remote hike seconds after getting multiple bee stings, he was the one who grabbed me by the shoulders, looked me in the eye, and reassured me, "You're okay. Everything is going to be fine."

It was just the reminder I needed.

He even wiped my tears and gave me a hug, in the stunning role reversal that starts to happen when your children are suddenly taller and stronger than you ever thought possible.

It's an honor to watch him grow and mature, confidently blazing his own path—one most people would avoid but that suits him perfectly.

Even if others don't recognize his struggles or value his incredible gifts, I see him. I've always seen him. I've been his mama for fifteen years, and I know in my bones that he, too, is going to be just fine.

Because, while everyone else is sitting around watching, my boy runs into the fire.

When Jacqueline Miller isn't worrying about her teens, she's writing about them. You can find her latest essays on Facebook.

Dear Daughter, You Are More than Your Body

DANIELLE SHERMAN-LAZAR

I remember every detail of the moment I found out the sex of my first child. The bright glow of the computer screen in the dark room. The cold seeping through my thin gown. The gentle touch as the sonographer spread warm gel on my growing belly. The feather-light pressure of the small wand. The way the air held in my lungs as I waited to hear the news.

Then the words came in a rush: "You're having a girl!"

"Wow, a girl," I repeated. Beside me, my husband gave my hand a firm squeeze.

But something lurked in the shadows beyond my joy, and I felt my excitement change to fear. It's not that I didn't want a girl—I just knew how hard it is to be a girl in this world.

The day of my sonogram, staring at the image of my baby on the screen and taking in her vital, living reality, I imagined the weight of her in my arms. I pictured her smiling eyes and dimpled cheeks. But I was terrified her innocence would become tainted, that she would arrive in this world only to be ripped apart by it.

You see, I have firsthand experience. Just three years earlier, I'd awakened in a hospital bed after having a seizure brought on by my eating disorder. I knew the difficulties this girl might face, and they overwhelmed me.

In that moment, my overriding fear was my daughter would somehow inherit an eating disorder from me. I know how deadly and all consuming an illness like this can be. I know the time I wasted over the course of two decades. I know the hurt I endured and how much of life—the beauty and the joy—I missed. And I knew I'd have to arm her with the tools necessary to fight the forces that would try to break her.

I knew I'd have to make my baby girl better, stronger, and empowered in every way I wasn't.

Five years later, I'm a mother to three daughters. What a gift it's been to be their mother and to learn and grow together.

Even though I'm in recovery, I still have days I look in the mirror and judge the woman staring back at me. I see a body that has changed three times over. There are stretch marks, spider veins, and a muffin top. Things don't fit quite the way they used to. But every mom has scars, cellulite, and excess skin. Our bodies aren't the same after bearing children, even if we manage to lose all the weight.

The truth is, we live in a culture that makes it hard to be a woman. When we're pregnant, our bellies are celebrated. But the second we give birth, we're expected to look as if we never carried babies. We're supposed to be moms without the effects of motherhood: thicker waist, wider hips, imperfect skin. Given that it's near impossible, is it any wonder mothers struggle?

But on the days I stand in front of the mirror checking my reflection a little longer than usual, I'll hear the pitter-patter of little feet running from behind and feel hands tugging my pants. My perspective shifts as the mirror fills with the images of my smiling children. They are reminders of my strength. Reminders of what matters.

They don't care about my body size. I'll never let them know I care either. They'll never hear me say my backside looks too big in these pants or that I feel ugly, even though there are days I feel nothing but. Children are like sponges, and if I'm filled with shame over my appearance, my daughters will soak it up. I won't let that happen.

I want to raise confident girls who aren't afraid to take up space. Girls who

SO GOD MADE A MOTHER

know they're so much more than their appearance. I work hard every day to do that. I compliment them on their kindness, intelligence, and courage over their appearance.

We don't own a scale in our house because I want my girls to know their worth is in who they are, not in how much they weigh. I know they'll doubt themselves at times. They're human and this world is hard, but I'll give them the tools to work through the challenges they face. I want them to experience life on their terms, and to do that, they need to be strong, resilient, and brave.

When I ask my daughter, "What makes you beautiful?" she answers, on cue, "My heart." And that's true for all of us, no matter how old we are.

Danielle Sherman-Lazar is a mom to four girls and a mental health advocate. She writes about both at *Living FULL*. Find her books on Amazon.

I Loved Them before I Knew Their Names

AMBER WATSON

I met them in my driveway on a summer night under the stars. A tired woman in a black minivan handed me a chubby nine-month-old baby boy. Then she went to the other side of the van and set free a sweet little toddler with a round face and dark, rebellious curls.

And just like that, our lives changed forever.

I met their baby sister in the hospital a day after she was born. She was so tiny I was scared to even breathe on her. She wrinkled her face as if she knew I didn't belong to her, but as long as I fed her, she didn't seem to mind. She was born fighting, and that spunkiness is evident to this day.

My path to becoming a mother began long before I met my children. It began in a cold doctor's office, where after sacrificing my dignity to several tests, I was told they didn't know why I wasn't able to get pregnant.

It began as a churning in my spirit when I heard about the hundreds of children in our area who needed loving foster homes.

It began at the dinner table one night when my husband and I discovered we'd been wrestling with the same calling.

It began when I made the decision to love them before I even knew their names.

It began when I made space in my heart and my home for little strangers to stay, even if only for a short time.

It began when I knew my love for these children would overwhelm me, torture me, and quite possibly ruin me, but that would never stop me from giving them the attachment they so desperately needed.

The secret ingredient along my journey to motherhood was—and still is—hope. It bubbled up inside me as I asked God to give us a family, however that might look.

I found it in the way those two little toddlers, who had been ripped away from everything they knew, somehow learned to trust my husband and me, two strangers who fumbled the ball many times as we learned to parent traumatized kids.

I cling to that hope when I wonder if I am enough for my children. *My children.* Sometimes I revel in the way that sounds.

These remarkable little beings have taught me so much about God and His abounding love and grace. In our daily lives, He continues to bring courage in the face of chaos and beauty from the grip of pain.

Is it a perfect story? Not at all. I'm not oblivious to the fact that another woman had to lose her children for me to gain my family. If you understand foster care, you know adoption is not the happy ending most people assume it to be. My children will grow up with questions I can't answer. I think about that a lot.

People often ask what happened to my children; they want to know why they were placed in foster care. The truth is, I probably don't even know the half of it, but it doesn't matter, because it's not my story to tell. My children will decide how and when they want to share their stories. But if you look closely, you can behold all that has taken place through them. The miracles speak for themselves.

My children are not defined by what has happened to them, nor by the circumstances life has dealt them . . . and neither are we. Isn't grace a beautiful thing?

My husband and I and our three little heroes were given a chance to make something whole out of our brokenness, and along the way, we became a family. It wasn't giving birth that made me a mother. Rather, loving my children has given birth to the mother my soul longed to be.

Amber Watson resides in Florida with her family. She started the blog *A Thing with Feathers* to share her journey of finding hope despite hardship.

Following
My Child's Lead

JACALYN WETZEL

There's something they don't prepare you for when you have kids. When a baby is born healthy and squealing its tiny little lungs out, everyone tells you how fast the time goes. They tell you that you need to memorize every second of these precious moments and every dimple in your new baby's hands. You hold your little bundle knowing how fleeting the time with them will be.

There's other advice that somehow rings true, though it's often more contradictory than beneficial, like, "Sleep when the baby sleeps" or "Hold them as much as they want to be held." While these things are meant to be helpful, they can leave a new parent paralyzed or, worse, feeling as if they're failing.

As the child ages, the advice changes, but it's always based on the typically developing child. No one tells you what to do when you have a child who may never fly the nest or when you have one who will fly a little (or a lot) later than their peers.

When my daughter was thirteen, she was diagnosed with autism. The breath still catches in my throat when I see *severe* in front of the diagnosis—the one that put the pieces together and shattered our world all at once. It wasn't that anything changed in this moment—it simply shattered our timelines and expectations. Suddenly I wasn't sure if she would have meaningful relationships outside our home. I questioned how her teachers and peers would treat her. I didn't know whether she'd get married one day and parent children of her own. I wondered how this diagnosis would alter the future I'd built for her in my mind.

It's a funny thing we do as parents when we have babies. We look at these tiny, perfect humans and lay the weight of our own expectations on their futures. Before they've even spoken their first words, we've married them off to our best friends' babies and started thinking about what vacations with our grandchildren will be like. It's mighty presumptuous of us, and it results in the disappointment of dreams that weren't ours to dream. Many parents would say they have no preconceived expectations for their children, but until you're face to face with a diagnosis, it's hard to know what's rolling around in the depths of your mind.

The day my daughter was diagnosed was the day my subconscious expectations surfaced. It was also the day we were both set free. I didn't know what to expect anymore, so I let her set the pace. I followed her lead and stepped in when needed. She was now the maker of her destiny, and I was her advocate.

Years have passed since then, and while she had difficulty maintaining certain friendships, I got to watch as friends embraced her with all her quirks. She was able to experience the gift of having other people, including strangers, advocate for her when she had trouble getting words out. She didn't miss homecoming or prom. She picked out dresses and danced the night away with a friend who turned out to be her saving grace in high school.

When she set her sights on art school, I trusted her. I had no idea the level of advocating I would have to do at every turn. There's no handbook on sending your autistic child to college. We tried two art schools before heading to community college. It was there she was able to continue to work on relational skills, social cues, and self-advocacy. We found the disability office and translated her IEP into college-level accommodations. We found resource centers and figured out ways to ask for help when you don't quite know what you're asking for. Still, there are some things that will just be late.

The beauty of watching her set her own timeline is that we get to stay in certain stages a little longer. While other parents are watching their newly graduated eighteen-year-olds move away from home, we get to hold on for a few extra years. I've been able to watch her turn into a person who knows exactly what she wants and isn't going to give up until she fulfills her dreams.

I didn't know if she would fly the nest one day, but she knew. She trusted herself, and I trusted her. And it has made our journey as mother and child that much sweeter.

Jacalyn Wetzel is an LCSW, a loving wife, and a mom of four great kids. She writes at *Jacalyn Wetzel*, which can be found on Facebook.

To My Rule-Following Firstborn

BREA SCHMIDT

×

I know I don't tell you enough what a good kid you are. As both the oldest and the rule follower, you seem to always fall victim to the attention I have to give your younger siblings, who are still in the "testing the waters" stage when it comes to rules.

While I try to keep your little sister from throwing her dinner on the floor, you quietly eat your entire meal before putting your dishes in the sink.

While I'm trying to calm your little brother's tantrum and get him in bed, you read silently in yours, having already put on your pajamas and brushed your teeth.

While I'm trying to wrangle a child who doesn't want to get into her car seat, you sit patiently in the back, already strapped into your booster.

While the little ones are arguing over a toy, you try to be the peacemaker as you kindly suggest they take turns.

So often you are doing what I ask of you. Being a good listener. Having patience. Choosing kindness. Using your manners. Being helpful around the house.

And I know sometimes it gets overlooked as I spend more time trying to put out fires and not enough time watering your beautiful spirit.

I don't mean for it to be this way. So today—every day—I want you to know I see you too.

I see you with the kind of empathy in your heart that could only be from God.

I see you with your fierce desire to bring happiness into our home and to the people around you.

I see you with your kindness when you ask me if you can help with the dishes or the vacuuming.

I see you with the respect you give to your family, your teachers, and your friends.

I see you being you.

And I hope you see me being me—someone who remembers being a kid like you, one who followed the rules and sometimes felt like that made her blend in.

I never want you to feel like you're not seen. I want to make sure you know how much your goodness makes you stand out and shine.

I'm proud of your big heart in a way I will never be able to describe. I'm not always perfect at showing that to you, but I'm vowing to do a better job.

I never want you to lose your inherent desire to do good, and I will love you through the days you get to those lines you'll inevitably choose to toe.

Most importantly, I want you to know I'm so proud to be your mom. I will make it my life's mission to help you hang on to your goodness by celebrating it every chance I can.

I love you,
Mom

Brea Schmidt is the speaker and writer behind the Pittsburgh-based social media community *The Thinking Branch*.

The
Acid-Washed
Epiphany

ELIZABETH ALLISON

×

The small, clenched fist foretold my doom.

"How about these, Devin?" I coaxed. "They look comfy, huh?"

He shook his head, and golden-brown strands swept over his eyes.

"But look how deep the pockets are," I insisted.

The disheveled seven-year-old scanned the pair he was clutching. "I like these."

A familiar suspicion began to gnaw at me. *This is so Devin. He doesn't want them—he just wants to disagree. Like he does with homework, dinner, bath time . . .*

I inhaled deeply and reminded myself that today, an afternoon of back-to-school shopping and lunch, was meant to be fun.

"Mm-kay." I sighed and soon found myself purchasing a pair of acid-washed jean shorts, a garish piece punctuated by chunky diagonal ruching along the front.

Determined that my son start second grade with *some* subtle pieces, I shopped for another hour with Devin, attending to his tales of Roblox woes and laughing at his corny animal jokes. At stop after stop, I pulled out an assortment of items: walking shorts, performance shorts, cargo shorts. He shook his head at each, and golden-brown wisps shook with it.

Button-up shirts, polo shirts, poplin shirts. He shook his head again.

Marvel tees, Mandalorian tees, Mario tees. He shrugged, then shook his head. I was sure he was trying to aggravate me. *This is so Devin,* I fumed silently.

Suddenly a cry ripped through the boys' department. "Baby Yoda!"

From a crammed rack, Devin excavated a crumpled tee and held it to his chest. Against an electric-blue background, four Warhol-inspired panels depicted the small creature in neon. Neon lemon. Neon pink. Neon lime. Neon gold. Bold, unabashed, dramatic—the shirt was so Devin.

My boy has always reveled in being different. Months ago, when I protested the intentionally mismatched knee-highs he donned for school, he asked why socks must be identical. I had no answer, and now this is Devin's signature look.

He has been taught timing and rhythm for years in drum class, but he delights in being dubbed "the crazy kid who improvises." When Devin wanted to demonstrate these skills at the school talent show, he practiced relentlessly and nailed his performance.

As we sat for lunch, Devin's curly locks fell wildly around his large, restless eyes. He spoke excitedly about the return to school in the fall, the rumors about second grade, and *the* shorts. "I've never seen anyone at school wear them."

"Uh-huh," I intoned mechanically, picking at my chopped salad.

"Mama," he implored.

I glanced up, and the dancing eyes stopped to look straight into mine. "*That's* why I like them."

That was it—the moment I saw my son for who he is—not some exhausting contrarian, not an attention-seeking clown. I saw a boy cultivating an individuality separate from me, separate from his brother, separate from his peers.

He returned to his mound of pasta, and I wondered, *Did I want to stand apart at that age?*

Devin returned my gaze and smiled.

No, I admitted. *I wanted to fit in.*

A mix of reverence and shame washed over me. Why had I been trying to constrain his thinking? Why had I discouraged the conspicuous shorts? Why had I directed him away from the pink pencil box? I'd told myself it was because life is hard enough without being different, but my son's echoing words had me reconsidering.

I thought of the artists I most appreciate—innovators who buck convention to create something new. I thought of my favorite writers—originators who embrace the unordinary. Suddenly my instinct to shield my son from being different felt backward. Don't those who think differently make us all better?

I thought of the boy at the park who, after being told his long hair made him look like a girl, shrugged off the insult. "Devin, did that hurt your feelings?" I had asked.

"Nah. Everyone should just look how they want."

My instinct to shield my son from being different suddenly seemed unnecessary. Aren't those who act differently already brave?

Pushing his long bangs from his eyes and over his left ear, he shoveled another forkful into his mouth, smiled through a smear of marinara sauce, and cocked his head.

"What's wrong, Mama?"

"Nothing. Just thinking."

"About what?"

I leaned toward the table. "I was thinking that I love how you want to be yourself."

His entire body pitched forward in a deep laugh, and the bangs fell back over his face. "Who else *would* I be, Mama?"

No one else. Of course, no one else.

Later, on the first day of school, Devin clambered out of the car and onto the curb in mismatched socks. As he frantically waved goodbye, making his tousled hair bounce against his electric-blue tee, I understood that I will always worry; I will always want to protect my son from getting hurt. But as he bounded through the front gate, I saw a boy who was confident, audacious, and happy.

And every day I give thanks that he is so Devin.

Elizabeth Allison is a former educator, fiction and nonfiction writer, and proud mother of two boys. Her work can be found on *The Write Profile*.

The Hellos and Goodbyes Are Hard Every Time

TIA HAWKINS

He is our low tide, like those shallow, beautiful waves you wait for all year. The ones that make you breathe in deep and refresh your soul. The ones that keep you calm and steady, no matter how anxious you were before you put your feet in them. The ones you set as your screen background and bring to mind when you need to feel a moment of peace in the chaos of life. That's home when he is here.

We have two tweens, and he still tucks them in. We joke that they're going to call him from college for his services.

He says yes when I say no—way more times than he should.

On the rare occasion he disciplines them, his eyes tear up.

His world revolves around them, and his around theirs.

He sends me chocolate-covered strawberries when I'm having a bad day.

He texts me every morning to see how I slept and to tell me he loves me.

He washes my clothes, because he has this wonderful obsession with the laundry.

He cleans. Like really cleans, with products.

He snuggles.

He carpools to dance and baseball, no matter how long his day was.

He never tells me no or questions my purchases (or my many, many deliveries).

He is the best gift giver, and his heart is huge.

I knew when we met he was already married to the military.

I knew when they called, he had to comply.

I knew he loved his career, and while I was welcome along for the ride, I could never stop it.

I knew we would be apart, but I definitely didn't know how much.

I knew I was independent and strong, but I didn't realize how dependent and weak I'd feel waiting on a single email.

I knew it would be hard, but I could never have imagined just how hard. Hard on me, hard on them, hard on him, hard on us.

I knew so much.

I knew so little.

Our family is made up of not just the four of us in this home but of an entire nation. Yes, he serves his country for us—but he serves it for you, too. He served for you before he even had us.

That's commitment.

That's honor.

That's duty.

We are well past the twenty-year mark of when he could retire, but that doesn't appear to be anywhere in sight. He has ranked up in promotions as far as he can go, yet he still puts on his uniform and boots every single morning.

Military life is hard, no matter how honorable it is. There's a constant wave of emotions, with no preparations and no pardons. No matter how proud or prepared you are, the tide will change—many times, with no warning.

Truthfully, I don't like it. I adjust to it.

The call has come, and he must go. The country needs him back, even though we need him too.

The tide is shifting again, and I can feel those waves of emotions changing with it. It builds a little higher every day, so I hold my breath . . . until he returns, and my breath returns with him.

Tia Hawkins's voice on mental health, motherhood, military life, and more can be found on her *Tea Talks with Tia* blog and social media platforms.

PART 3

SO GOD MADE A MOTHER

known

✕

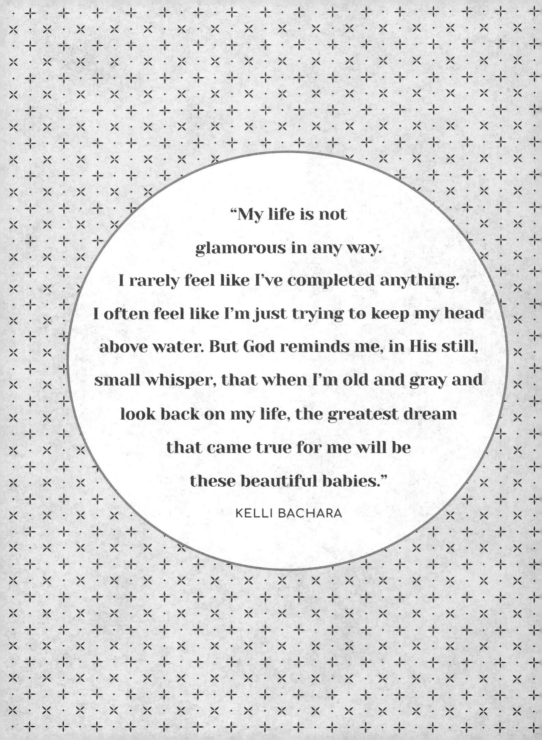

"My life is not glamorous in any way. I rarely feel like I've completed anything. I often feel like I'm just trying to keep my head above water. But God reminds me, in His still, small whisper, that when I'm old and gray and look back on my life, the greatest dream that came true for me will be these beautiful babies."

KELLI BACHARA

The Look

LESLIE MEANS

✕

I saw her out of the corner of my eye. She was smiling subtly, maybe even smirking, but she had *the look* on her face. You might know that look. The one with the pursed lips and the tilted head and the expression screaming, *Please get control of your kid.*

I'm familiar with this look from strangers—and during one season of my life, it made me furious.

I know my kid is running around this grocery store like a hyper hyena, I would say to myself. *I know I should be a better parent. I know this isn't proper. I know, I know, I know. But I'm tired. And I have to make dinner. And we have to pay bills. And I just want to get home, get this kid fed, and put him in bed so I can relax for ten dang minutes.*

I've been there. But I know better now.

I have three kids: Ella, Grace, and their little brother, Keithan. He is my wild child, as they say. He's the one who will, on occasion, run around the grocery store begging for toy cars and cheese and ice cream and all the things a rambunctious little boy finds delightful.

Sometimes he is well behaved. But today was not that day.

"Keithan! Get over here right now," I scream-whispered down the candy aisle. You know the scream-whisper, right? Where you're trying to get the kid's attention without screaming in your loudest voice but where you're still loud enough to drown out the early-nineties music playing over the store speakers?

"But, Mom," he yelled, "I just want this toy. Can I have this toy?"

"Nope," I told him. I've learned no is a very good answer.

And that's when I saw her. The older woman, likely in her seventies, who gave me the look. Our eyes met for just a moment, and instead of getting sad or angry, I smiled at her. And she smiled back.

That was it.

I didn't know this stranger. I assume she's a mother—I could read it in her face. Many years ago, when I was just starting out in this parenting gig, her look would have made me cry tears of exhaustion and sadness. But this time, I knew it meant something more.

I knew, because I give that same look in grocery store aisles.

When a mom is holding a crying baby.

When a mom is frustrated with a cranky toddler.

When a mom is standing in the hair aisle, picking out pretty things for her little girl.

I give them a look too. It's not a look of judgment—it's a look of compassion and nostalgia. A moment from mom to mom. A single glance to say, *Hey, I've been there. You're doing a great job. It's all going to be okay. Just love those babies—time goes so fast.*

I strapped Keithan into his car seat, gathered the rest of the groceries from my cart, and made my way into the driver's seat. And that's when I cried.

Because I know soon—so soon—I'll be that seventy-year-old woman giving a look to a thirty-nine-year-old mom, begging for just one more minute with my hyper little boy.

There's magic in those little moments we feel truly seen as moms. Whether it's a smile from a stranger or an unexpected "I love you" traced in the steam of your bathroom mirror, those moments strengthen us.

They remind us we're not mothering on an island of exhaustion and self-doubt. They connect us to one another—mom to mom, heart to heart.

I hope you'll feel seen and known as you read these next several stories—and encouraged too. Because you're a great mom. Don't ever forget it.

I'm Holding
My Dreams in My Arms

KELLI BACHARA

If I wrote a list of all the things I'd like to accomplish in my life, it would be long. Really long.

I have a lot of dreams I hope to bring to fruition, God willing. It seems like new ideas and desires come to my mind often. I'd love to write a book, start a moms' group, get a business up and running, create a workout regime, redo my whole house, and so much more.

I'll be thinking about these big, beautiful dreams, and then I'll snap back to reality when I get smacked in the face with a toy or see my kids fighting in the other room or hear someone yelling, "Mommy!"

So I hit pause on my dreams and go back to doing mom things.

As I wipe bottoms, dole out snacks, sing lullabies, and try to keep everyone sane, my big, shiny dreams get placed on a shelf in the back of my mind.

I realize I can't do it all. All those ideas that seem so glamorous, so passion filled—I literally don't have the time or energy for them. Not when I'm in the thick of motherhood like this.

The truth is, motherhood means I have to put some of these dreams on hold. I don't have the freedom to do all the things I want to do.

The other day when I was rocking my little one, I was thinking about those dreams way up on the shelf of my brain, and I heard a small voice say, *You are living your dream right now.*

So many emotions flooded my heart as I looked at my kids and the mess all around.

My life is not glamorous in any way. I rarely feel like I've completed anything. I often feel like I'm just trying to keep my head above water.

But God reminded me, in His still, small whisper, that when I'm old and gray and looking back on my life, the greatest dream that will have come true for me will be these beautiful babies.

No other accomplishment of my life will even come close. I get to live in this fulfilled dream, right this moment.

Yes, I'm allowed to dream about doing things besides being a mom, and I will absolutely chase them someday.

But these kids of mine are not an inconvenience. They are not a burden. They are not a disturbance to my life. They are a dream come true.

So as I look at my little loves, I thank God for the beautiful reminder He spoke to me: I am not putting my dreams on hold. Right now, I'm holding my dreams in my arms.

Kelli Bachara, writer for *The Unraveling Blog,* loves to encourage women by reminding them how loved and cared for they are by God.

Love Is Born
in the Waiting

AMANDA McCOY

※

Strapped down in a Jesus pose, I am aware of my nakedness. The room is full of people and voices, but I've never felt so alone. I know what's to come—the violence and the blood. I know they will cut the baby from my body, just as they've done twice before. I never wanted this type of birth. But slowly I feel the resentment and anger begin to slip away.

I surrender. I am breathing. I am waiting for them to begin. A doctor is whispering in my ear, asking if I feel okay. I feel sick. I feel sad. I feel anxious. I shiver. I tell him I'm fine.

My husband is next to me. A man of few words, he doesn't say much, and for once, I'm grateful. He holds my hand and I squeeze it hard, hoping he understands but knowing he can't. He is perfect in this moment, knowing I need his touch, not his words.

My heart races as they begin. I hear them, but it's as if I'm underwater, their voices muted and distorted. I stare at the ceiling and try not to think about my arms strapped down, about how naked I am.

I can tell they are cutting me open; I feel my skin tugging and pulling. My heart thuds. It takes too long. I wait.

When they pull her from me, I feel the lift—a sudden lightness. A liberation. I am just me again. I have longed to be free of the baby, of her weight, for months. I have been desperate for this moment, but now that she's gone, she's all I want.

She releases a strangled, startled newborn cry, and the doctors and nurses *ooh* and *aah*. They talk about her—about her hair, about how beautiful she is. I remain alone behind the curtain, unable to see her. I close my eyes and wait.

I tell my husband to leave me, to go to the baby. He asks if I'm sure, and I nod. He goes.

I feel like my heart might burst. I panic, my breath shallow and fast, and a nurse tries to calm me. She shushes me as if I'm a child. In my head, I repeat over and over, *Please, bring me the baby.*

They take the baby to the weigh station to get her vitals and clean her up. I turn my head to see her, but she's too far away. There are too many people. There is so much noise.

My husband appears, and I blink back tears. He's talking about her, how perfect she is. His voice is warm and full and excited. He asks if I'm okay. My stomach somersaults and flips.

I tell him I'm fine.

They're sewing me up, putting me back together. A voice is counting over and over, checking the instruments to make sure they aren't leaving something inside me. I want to tell them I'm empty, as empty as can be.

They are pushing on me, yanking and tugging. A young doctor climbs on top of my body, and I sense her weight without really feeling it, the sensation surreal and bizarre. She pushes the blood from my body with her hands and her knees. She leaves a deep bruise that lingers for weeks, fading from purple-black to green-yellow. A reminder of how my baby had to enter this world.

Please, bring me the baby. Please.

They announce the baby's weight and length, and still she cries. My body aches for her.

I crane my neck to see my husband holding her. I feel my heart hitch and lurch. They are talking to me, telling me how well I did. I nod. I want to ask why my body failed me, why I had to birth her this way, why I have to wait to hold her. But I say nothing.

My husband brings the baby to me, and I see her for the first time—with her red hair and perfect, tiny fingers. My voice catches in my throat. I speak to her, my baby, and I long to touch her, to press her against my body. My husband tilts her so I can kiss her cheek, the most I can manage while strapped down like this.

He takes her away, and then the nurse wheels her out of the room. She's gone. I feel sick and dizzy, as if I might throw up. I breathe in and out.

The voice continues to count, ensuring all the instruments are accounted for. I begin counting in my head along with the voice, finding solace in the repetition. I wait.

They're covering me up, pulling down the curtain, freeing my arms. Things are moving fast now. They count to three and lift me onto another gurney. They place warming blankets on me. I am comforted by the weight.

I wait for the baby in a new room. My husband sits by my side and messages our families on his phone. He smiles, happy to be a father again.

I can't feel anything from the waist down. I wait and wonder if I'm less of a mother because my babies had to be cut from my body. Nurses come in periodically to check my vitals and ensure I'm fine.

I am here, but I am not. Part of me is outside my body, in another room, as it will be from now on. Part of me will always live in my children, inside their beating hearts.

I won't feel whole until my daughter is in my arms, until I feel her skin against my skin, until her heart thrums against mine. Only then will I be fine.

Amanda McCoy lives in Ohio with her family and rescue dogs. Her blog *The Write McCoy* features raw and real writing about motherhood and marriage.

The Things
They Don't Tell You

REBECCA COOPER

✕

You find out you're about to have a baby, and suddenly your Amazon cart is full of books. You start with *What to Expect When You're Expecting*, but as the list grows, it starts to look like a cry for help, because what in the world have you gotten yourself into?

You see the thin lines on a pregnancy test, and all at once you feel the weight of responsibility. You are now responsible for so much more than just yourself, and that's the first thing no one can explain to you.

Not your mom.

Not your nana.

Not your best friend.

The weight of the being inside of you is more than just ounces and pounds— it's so much heavier. The responsibility is found in the spaces between the things they do tell you.

"You'll be such a good mom," they coo at baby showers while holding tapas and lemonade. "You'll be so patient and loving. We can't wait to see you as a mama."

You picked up a random pamphlet at the doctor's office, and now you're researching the HPV vaccine, realizing you'll have to talk to your daughter one day about periods and permission, and you'll whisper to your spouse about the little girl they found down by the river two summers ago. You put your head on his shoulder, and something shifts way down in the very essence of who you are. How do you keep her safe every day for the rest of her life?

"Have you decided on godparents?" They greet you, smiling, at church, and you nod your head like it's the most solemn decision you'll ever make. "I'm sure you'll make the right choice."

Amniocentesis, induction, Pitocin, postpartum. You learn so much so fast it feels like an assault. You stay awake at night and worry about autism and listeria found in lunch meat and whether baby laundry soap is necessary. Pillows out of the crib, blankets out of the crib, nothing hanging over the crib—and the truth is sometimes none of that even matters, because you slipped up on a Thursday morning and read the statistics on SIDS while sitting at your desk.

They don't tell you how you'll have to look at your doctor at your forty-week appointment and whisper to him that if it comes down to it, he should save the baby first. You blink in surprise at the conviction you hear in your voice. You didn't read about that in any of the books from Amazon.

"What's the theme for the first birthday party?" Your mother is trying to make conversation on a Tuesday. *He's ONE-derful* bangs around in your head, and . . . he really is.

Does Miss Sarah spend enough time rocking him at daycare? Does he get fed enough? Changed enough? Do they talk to him, play with him, and pick him up when he cries?

You blend baby food made from carrots you pulled from your own backyard, and you realize not one person has thought to warn you about the random four-hour fevers that come and go or about the looks you'll get when you just can't get your baby to stop crying at the grocery store. They don't tell you how your body will tremble with division—one side of you will be full of frustration and the other will be full of piercing protection for the little in your arms.

They don't tell you how it will sweep over you in an instant, this realization. You will hold him in your suddenly sweaty arms until the Second Coming if you have to, because you are his mother. And this is what mothers do.

"What size pants should I grab for a Christmas gift?" Your grandma's raspy voice greets you over the phone.

Growth curves and head size and weight supplements . . . and is he small for his class? Is he eating okay? Why won't he eat his vegetables? Motherhood is an endless stream of self-inflicted, unanswerable questions. He's on his third ear infection of the year, and nobody—not one single person—has fallen over dead from a kick to the kidney in the middle of the night by a sick six-year-old, but you're so tired you think it may be possible.

They don't tell you how your eyes will burn in the grocery store because you haven't slept in six years, and they don't tell you your ears will roar and that sometimes your dinner will be microwave popcorn, because they also forget to tell you that your needs come last.

"Is your daughter going to try out for choir this fall?" Her teacher is trying to make conversation at open house. Your mouth opens, then closes.

They don't ever tell you about the heartache either. They don't warn you about the pit in your stomach when you see your baby playing alone for the first time or when their name doesn't appear on the final roster. They don't tell you about the ache you'll feel when they're frustrated on a Monday night because they just can't understand photosynthesis or the Pythagorean theorem or allusions in *Romeo and Juliet*.

They don't warn you their losses are your losses too. They don't tell you their tears are also yours, their hurts are also yours, their long, broken days are also yours. They don't tell you the personalities they try on like new shoes will also be your puzzles to decipher or how their exploration will be yours to navigate as well.

"Where is your son going to college?" Linda from down the street was at your baby shower. She watched him grow up.

And they don't warn you about the joy that gurgles deep in your chest nearly every single day. They don't tell you how you will love your child with every sinewy fiber of your holy being. They don't tell you how you will love in the most unexplainable, inconceivable, full, and whole kind of way. They don't tell you how the sleepless nights and the late nights helping with homework and the hard bleacher nights and the drive-thru dinner nights—they're all somehow worth it. They don't tell you how you'll feel as though an extension of you is just walking around and their happiness is somehow your happiness, and did you even know?

Perhaps they don't tell you on purpose. Perhaps they let the surprise of motherhood roll over you in waves because they know what you are only just realizing: it's the greatest adventure and the greatest gift you'll ever be given.

Rebecca Cooper is a mom, a lover of nachos and Jesus, and she lives every day rooted in joy. Find her latest books on Amazon.

As a Mom of Four Black Sons, This Is What I Pray

KIERRA TATE HENDERSON

✕

I am completely enamored with my four sons. We boy moms have a reputation for being a little crazy, and who can blame us? Having all boys is like being a resident queen—everyone practices their chivalry on you. My husband, Paul, takes his commitment to train his boys to be gentlemen quite seriously.

My first son, PJ, who is eight, opens the car door for me, even when I'm getting in the driver's seat.

My second son, Joey, who is six, likes to bring me ice-cold glasses of water.

My third son, David, who is four, likes to kiss my hand every time I leave the house.

And my fourth son, Noah, who is one, has the hug of a koala bear. When he rests his face on my shoulder, I am undone.

I like to think such chivalry is compensation for the furniture that has been abused, for the ceiling fans and curtains that have broken, and for the smells. Oh, the smells! The fragrance of flatulence adorns their presence, and I can hardly ever escape it.

Still, like a true boy mom, I think my sons are precious.

My boys look so much alike, but each has his own color. I like to boast that I have a son in every flavor I love. There's one for peanut butter, one for honey, and one for brown sugar. I prayed for my youngest son to be the color of milk chocolate, and he is—his skin looks like melting chocolate, sticky and smooth and sweet.

But every once in a while, when I'm smiling at his chocolatey-brown skin, my admiration is interrupted by a fearful thought. Suddenly the names and faces of Black men and boys parade across my mind—men and boys who died unjustly while doing normal things like jogging, playing with a toy, or walking down the street wearing a hoodie and eating candy.

In my anguish, I ask myself, *Did I make a mistake in asking God for such a dark-skinned son? Will the richness of his melanin cause him to be more readily stereotyped, judged, or profiled? Will he be an easy target of racism, both covert and overt? God, what did I ask for?*

Sometimes I find myself ruminating on what it's like for white moms raising white sons. I wonder what it would be like knowing society was built favoring my son's success and protection. Or would it even occur to me?

I constantly reassure myself my prayer for a chocolate-skinned son wasn't a mistake or something to regret. And if God is so faithful to answer my prayer for the way I wanted my son to look, how much more faithful will He be to take care of him? So I keep praying. Just like my grandma's prayers kept me, my prayers will keep my boys.

Dear mama, I want to give you a glimpse into my prayers so I can give you a glimpse into my heart. This is so you can pray with me, so you can change with me. And though I hope people will, in fact, change, I can't expect them to. My hope is only in Jesus, who is forever faithful.

As a mom of four Black sons, this is what I pray:

Lord, protect my boys and my husband—bring them home safely.
　　Please give them wisdom about how to speak to those in authority.
　　Father, don't let any man be afraid of them, and don't let them be afraid of any man. Let them walk in power, love, and a sound mind.
　　Let Your justice work on their behalf in everything they do.
　　Lord, I pray they will always be bold and never shrink to make others feel comfortable. I pray they will not conform to any culture in

order to be deemed safe and acceptable. Give them the sense of liberty that allows them to be exactly who You created them to be.

Lord, if I look at the world as it is, the odds are stacked against them. But I pray their gifts will make room for them. I pray You will open doors for them that no one can close.

I pray they will receive compassion and understanding in their challenges and not be labeled, stigmatized, or mistreated because of them.

And God, if my sons are ever truly wrong, have mercy. Don't let others rejoice in their wrongdoings. Let them forgive and be forgiven.

I pray my boys will believe they are beautiful and intentional masterpieces who bear Your image. Remind them they are princes and heirs to Your Kingdom.

Lord, please let my boys live out all their days. Let them live to create a godly legacy. Let them live to be loving husbands, fathers, and grandfathers. Thank You for letting them live so they can accomplish Your perfect plan.

And I pray they will love as You do, no matter what.

In Jesus' name, amen.

Kierra Tate Henderson is a wife and a mother to four boys. She's the creator of *Beloved Mama* and founder of the I AM MAMA movement.

The Sting
of Invisible
Paper Cuts

KATE SWENSON

X

The other day over coffee, I chatted with a mom whose daughter had just been diagnosed with autism, among other labels. Epilepsy. Language disorder. The list was far too long for a little girl who wears a pink tutu and pigtails. This mom was looking to me for help. She wanted someone to give her the answers, the secrets. To fill her with hope and take away the worry she carried.

I mostly just listened, because that's what I needed seven years ago when my son was diagnosed with autism.

As she spoke about her fight, I was transported back to those early days, before we really knew. The denial. Then appointments. The questions: *Am I doing enough?* The strain on my marriage, my career, my relationships. The waiting.

Then getting the folder. How it was slid across the table as if it held the secrets to our future. *Autism spectrum disorder.* The send-off, with little more than "Good luck." The drive home and feeling like so much had changed from just hours before.

And finally, the fight of my life. The one I had to suit up for every single day. It was invisible to everyone else, but I was at war. I wore armor only parents with a child like mine can understand.

As this mom spoke about trying to find resources and support, I listened. I felt the ache in my own chest as she tried to convince herself of the realities she could see but not accept . . . not yet.

I realized I'm starting to forget the ache. The longing. The hoping and the wondering. I can suppress it now, because it has been replaced with the only thing stronger: joy.

My son is happy. And he is exactly who he is supposed to be. He is Cooper.

For eight years I searched for something. Help. Hope. Easy. Typical, even. What I should have been searching for was joy—his joy. And now, over time, that joy has turned to gratitude. How grateful am I to have this child in my life who shows me the way.

I listened as she spoke, then told her how wonderful it will be when she gets through this hard part—the hard part that will drag on for years and turn her inside out. But she will make it through, and eventually she will become the person and mother she was meant to be all along. The person after.

She wasn't ready to hear all that yet. I wasn't either, not for years. And there's no rushing the process. There's no magic pill. It's a journey—one that deserves grace.

Later, as I pulled into my driveway, I saw a dozen kids playing football in the yard across the street. All ages were there—boys and girls. It was like a scene out of a 1950s neighborhood.

Then I heard a little girl yell, "Can Sawyer play?" As I stood there watching, a neighborhood boy, a fourth grader, joined the group. He looked so much like Cooper they could have been twins. He was running and shouting and playing.

And for a second, I remembered. The sting of what-if, like a dozen paper cuts right on the surface of my skin. It wasn't visible to the naked eye, but it was enough to take my breath away.

Tears flooded my eyes. *What if . . . ?* What if my son were able to run from house to house and play? What if he could ride a bike? What if he could join in a game of football?

I'm starting to forget. But I still go back to the other world sometimes—to the place I thought we'd be.

I shut the garage door and went inside. Cooper was waiting for me, like he always is whenever I return home. I engulfed him in the biggest bear hug and smiled at his backward shirt. Holding my hand, he brought me to the computer to show me the book he wants for his birthday. It's an old train guide—the one we already have a dozen copies of. He wants one more.

He giggled when I reminded him he has weeks to wait until his birthday. I know he will ask me a hundred more times today. And that's okay. I'm happy to answer.

I let that smile of his soothe the sting. I am covered in paper cuts, I think. Maybe all parents are—I don't know. They are invisible to the eye. Scarred over, even. But they won't let me fully forget.

So let the joy of a happy, beautiful life carry you through. And let the gratitude that comes with being part of something special dull the sting. And whenever you can, be there for the other mothers—the new ones who haven't started to forget yet. Because that's your gift to give.

Kate Swenson is the author of *Forever Boy*, creator of *Finding Cooper's Voice*, and tour guide to her amazing son Cooper.

Yes, Angels
Ride the Bus

KATHY RADIGAN

×

I hung up the phone, my hand frozen on the receiver. I hadn't realized I was holding my breath until I heard my loud sigh. It spoke of defeat, exhaustion, and a shattered heart.

Our second attempt at medical intervention had failed. I sat at my desk doing my best to process the information our fertility doctor had just given me. The previous month, I'd had my fourth miscarriage in thirteen months.

I knew my hormone levels were proving to be a real problem. I now had a second uterine biopsy to prove it. I wasn't just a three-time loser in the pregnancy game. I was now a four-time failure.

The doctor said we could try one more month on this protocol if we wanted to, but moving forward, we would have to get more aggressive and try IVF. I hadn't said this to the doctor yet, but my husband, Joe, and I had decided we weren't going any further. At least not for now. We were burned out.

We had hoped a little medical intervention by one of the top fertility doctors in Manhattan would be the answer. It wasn't. Joe said he felt like we were playing the tables at Vegas each month. We were desperate for our number to come up, only to be destroyed when we lost. I didn't want to admit it, but he was right. We were stuck in a pattern we had no control over.

I couldn't go on like this anymore. I dreaded speaking to my family. I didn't want to hear my mom tell me one more time that God had a plan or see my sisters' veiled frustration over why I couldn't stop obsessing over having a baby and enjoy my very nice life.

I didn't want to hear from my friends anymore either. They were all knee-deep in babies, kids, and healthy pregnancies. I was flooded with envy and anger, which in turn made me feel guilty.

This wasn't me. I'm not an angry person by nature. Usually I'm thrilled to see others thrive and fulfill their dreams, yet in this area I felt powerless.

My anger grew with every step on my way to the hospital after work. My soul was weary. I wasn't just mad at God—I was furious. Why did my babies have to die? Why did everyone else get their happy ending and we didn't? We'd done everything right. We'd been married five years, our relationship was strong, and we both had good jobs, health insurance, and money in the bank. And now we even had a house with a little room we'd painted for a nursery.

This wasn't even remotely fair. My anger grew with every step on my way to the bus stop. Why had God forgotten me? I was at the lowest point I'd ever been.

And that's when I met an angel. No, she didn't have wings or a heavenly glow. She was just an ordinary woman I'd ridden the bus with a few times. I had enjoyed our few conversations in the past, but since she had two kids and worked part time, I didn't see her often.

She gave me a gentle smile. "You look how I feel."

"Yeah, it's not a good day," I said. And with that, the tears I'd been stifling came to the surface.

I noticed she looked upset too. "Not a great day for you, either?"

"No, I think this was one of the worst professional days I've ever had."

We spoke the whole ride home. I talked about my deep yearning for a child and how everything we were doing wasn't working. I shared the ugly feelings plaguing my heart, from the resentment and anger to the guilt and helplessness. She spoke of her work frustration and how hard it was to combine her career and her kids. She felt she was letting them both down.

I don't remember either of us saying anything particularly profound, but at

SO GOD MADE A MOTHER

the end of our ride, I felt better. Lighter. When the bus came to our stop, we got off, hugged each other, and went our separate ways.

As I walked the two blocks to my house, I decided we needed to try one more time on this protocol, just for me. If it didn't work, we would stop treatment. I was tired of being angry and jealous. I needed to work on myself a bit.

For the next month, I did a prayer vigil. Each day I visited a church on my lunch hour for a few minutes and asked for guidance and peace.

That was a turning point. My healing started, and though at the end of the month I wasn't pregnant, I felt ready to move on. Joe and I decided to look into adoption, and I opened up to the idea of a life without children. I found a church I loved and felt ready to welcome possibilities in a way I hadn't in years. Joy was creeping back into my life.

I didn't see my bus friend again for about six months. Then one morning, as I made my way to the bus stop, she happened to be there with her husband and their two kids.

We happily greeted each other, then her eyes landed on my swollen belly. She gave me a quizzical look. "Are you . . . ?"

"Five months." I beamed. "We're having a boy."

A bright smile spread across her face. She pulled me into her arms for a warm embrace. Time rolled on, and I had my beautiful son Thomas, my firstborn. Eventually, we added two more babies to our family, Elizabeth and Peter.

That was the last time I saw my friend. Twenty-three years later, I still hold her in my heart, and I will always be grateful. She came to me at just the right time, exactly when I needed an angel.

Kathy Radigan created the blog *My Dishwasher's Possessed*. Her writing has been featured on numerous online publications, including viral posts for *HuffPost* and *Scary Mommy*.

I Met My Dad after He Died

ALYSE BRESSNER

Mozzarella sticks and a milkshake—that's what I ordered every other Sunday when my dad took my sister and me out for lunch at the local diner.

It wasn't because I particularly loved mozzarella sticks and milkshakes, but because they were the quickest items on the menu. If I ordered those instead of a burger, we could be in and out in under an hour, and I wouldn't have to see him again for another two weeks.

My parents divorced when I was twelve, and I was relieved when it happened. In fact, that's what I'd asked my mom for. I have very few childhood memories of my dad, and the ones I do have are more like feelings. From a young age, I remember feeling angry, resentful, embarrassed, and uncomfortable around him.

At just six years old, I knew my dad wasn't like my friends' dads. I'll never forget Alexis, a girl at the daycare center I attended. She constantly talked about her dad, and I remember him vividly. In his perfectly tailored suit, he was tall and handsome, with dark, slicked-back hair parted to the side. Every evening when he walked through those doors, Alexis would stop whatever she was doing and run to him in a full-on sprint. He would open his arms, hug her, and twirl her around like it was the best part of his day. And every evening, my six-year-old heart would sink, knowing I would never have a dad like that.

What I had was a dad who became irate over a spilled glass of milk. A dad who made himself scarce during family vacations. A dad who often went to bed before dinner was even on the table. A dad who couldn't take care of himself, let alone his children.

That is the narrative I told myself as I made my way through adolescence and into adulthood. For years, those every-other-Sunday lunches were filled with surface-level small talk and an abundance of silence. For years, his occasional phone calls were awkward and rushed. For years, he could barely muster a smile in my presence. The bimonthly visits eventually turned into once-a-year events after I left for college and then moved a few hours away to pursue my career. But even once a year felt like too much.

Then I gave birth to my son and a new identity: motherhood. As a parent, I felt the immense weight of my new responsibility. I experienced anxiety like never before, yet it was familiar. It was my dad. All the parts I hated about him abruptly surfaced in my own life.

For years, I'd believed his mental health issues were a choice. As a child, I believed I should have been enough to pull him from the depths of his deep depression and overwhelming anxiety. I believed he'd purposely chosen a life of dejection because it was easier than being a present and loving father. Yet there I was, with my perfect infant son, wondering why this beautiful child wasn't enough to pull me out of my own despair.

As children, we put our parents on pedestals. Even into adulthood. Even when they've proven they don't belong there. Even when they don't *want* to be there. And when we continue to hold them there, we're crushed by the weight of disappointment when they fail to meet our idealistic expectations over and over again.

I'd spent so many years looking up at my dad through a cloud of exhausted expectations. So at age twenty-eight, I took my dad down from that pedestal. I gained a different vantage point, a new perspective. My childhood started to make more sense as I attempted to love him where he was. He would no longer be the sorrow in my story but a hopeful revelation.

As I began to see him like never before, I realized the father I knew was a shell of his former self. He was broken in so many ways, and I had so many regrets, so much guilt for the way I'd treated him all those years. How much had I added to his suffering when, as a disgruntled teenager, I refused to hug him? How much more pain had I caused him when I ignored his phone calls?

I told myself there was time. I told myself that before he died, we would have the opportunity for a long goodbye. I told myself all our tattered loose ends would be neatly tied up—someday.

That someday never came. On a cold January morning, at the age of sixty-two, my dad died unexpectedly from a massive heart attack. In the days following his death, I was met with more things I didn't expect.

The walls of his house were lined with framed photos of my sister and me over the years; the end tables were cluttered with pictures of our kids. He had kept every single birthday card, Father's Day card, and Christmas card I'd ever sent him. He had over a dozen prayer books and Bibles, and between the wrinkled pages of the most well-loved one was a preschool photo of me along with his place card from my wedding: "Dad, Table 5."

Those days after my dad's death, while beautiful, were also astonishingly difficult. I felt a soul-crushing sadness, interwoven with guilt and regret.

"I love you, Alyse. With my whole heart."

That's how he ended his last voicemail to me. And that's what I'd gotten wrong all those years. He had always loved me with his whole heart. Every detail of his life said so.

I met my dad after he died. I finally saw him not for who I wanted him to be but for who he truly was: a broken but beautiful man with a heavy cross to bear—and quite possibly the proudest father the world has ever known.

Alyse Bressner is a Midwest mom of two. She shares an authentic view of stumbling through life, marriage, and motherhood on her blog, *She Writes Flowers*.

The Mushroom

ADELLE PURDHAM

✕

I walk with my dog to the top of the gravel driveway, where it's flat. I'm meandering, thinking about my day, while my rust-colored, seven-month-old vizsla pup tears ahead of me, then falls behind, nose to the ground.

I pivot at the top of the long drive, as I usually do, and with the next step, I catch sight of a magnificent mushroom. Its top reminds me of a Frisbee, flat and round. I'm marveling at it—its shape and size, and the very fact of its being—when my vizsla glides by me and, with one careless step, topples the fungus, leaving its fragile stem snapped at the base.

In an instant, the mushroom I admired is destroyed, its life obliterated. My immediate reaction is one of partial regret and wonder. Partial, in that I am not overly attached to this mushroom; regret, because the mushroom will no longer grow due to the chance encounter with my dog and me.

I also wonder at my own reaction. Is it anger? Disappointment? I feel conflicted emotions toward the mushroom for not defending itself better. *Now why would you go and grow a flimsy neck like that when you have such a big head?* I blame the victim. The mushroom was brave enough to grow in the heart of the driveway, but why would it do such a thing? Why didn't it hide, protect itself better? It's a wonder a toadstool can survive at all with wild animals stalking around, cutting them down with the graze of their bare knees. What a delicate life the fungi lead.

But are we so different?

I'm angry at the mushroom, but perhaps I'm also angry at myself for being part of the destruction, for being vulnerable in my own right. I, too, hold a large and heavy head atop a flimsy neck . . . could it snap one day? Or is it my maternal instinct kicking in, grieving the loss of a life in a way only a mother who has played a role in creating it can?

That night at bedtime, I'm in charge, and chaos breaks loose. I promise a story as a bribe to the first girl in bed. My youngest is writhing on the floor. My middle child is upset, and my oldest lies patiently in bed, silently praising herself for being first, because I have lost the energy and will to do so. We are on month 5,008 or thereabouts of sticking close to home, and parental patience is wearing thin. *Translucent* may be a better word.

I lie on my stomach on top of my eldest daughter's quilt, and she requests a continuation of a story I told her about a saber-tooth tiger. I can barely remember what I had for dinner, let alone a tiger story I made up over a month ago, so instead I describe a bland version of real life and kids going back to school.

My daughter reaches up and presses my cheeks with both hands. "Bad story," she complains.

"Don't touch my face, please." I am not in the mood.

I move to the next room, where my daughter Elyse is audibly complaining about I-have-no-idea-what and my youngest is crying for her story. "I wanted to be first!"

"But you'll get the last story," I promise her. "The last story's better. I'll make it the best one."

"Hey!" my oldest complains from the other room.

I sit on the edge of my youngest daughter's bed and look at Elyse, who has Down syndrome. She's slumped on her bed like a tired dandelion in her yellow pajama top.

"Do you want a snuggle?" I ask.

"Yeah."

I'm surprised she agrees. She's a big-time Daddy's girl, especially at bedtime.

I gather her in my arms, recalling the line of poetry by Kim Fahner I read earlier in the day: "Gather me in now / For my heart is lost." She rests her chin on my shoulder.

My daughter is seven, nearly eight, but her eyelids droop and she falls asleep in my arms, as she's done since she was an infant. She relaxes into me, and then she's gone, fast asleep.

In that moment, something about her fragility, her dependence on me reminds me of the mushroom—the one we killed. Does having Down syndrome set her apart, like that lone spindly stalk? Does it put her at risk of being kicked, toppled over?

Why is it that I shy away from vulnerability? Why does it cause anger to rise inside me, making me wish my kids were tougher? Is this some form of protection, some attempt at self-preservation, a shield I've forged around my family and myself? *Bad things wouldn't have happened*, I think, *if you'd planned ahead, picked a better patch of grass, changed the way you're grown.*

And that's it, isn't it? My daughter can't change the way she was grown. She was born in the middle of the path, with a big head and a flimsy stalk. She's at risk. When we got her diagnosis, we heard a lot about the "risk" of carrying a fetus with Down syndrome. *A risk to what or to whom?* I wondered. I wasn't sure during pregnancy, but now I see the risk is the other way around. My daughter is the one who is constantly put in harm's way by society's perceptions of her value.

I gently lower Elyse from my embrace back onto her bed. She stirs, but her arms remain raised, half-bent above her head, as though she were praying. She is as peaceful as can be, and I'm happy to have given her what she needs. While she looks physically flimsy at first glance, her slumbering spirit is strong. She is alive and worthy—as worthy as I'll ever be as her mother.

A month later, I walked back to that same spot with my dog. I left without finding even a trace of the large mushroom, as though it never existed. In its place I found clusters of tiny mushrooms, earth toned and thriving, and I couldn't help but wonder if this is a lot like life. Nothing is wasted.

Everything—and everyone—serves a purpose. Life has a way of sprouting up in unexpected places.

Now I am grateful for the mushrooms, mindful of them. And I am extra careful where I step.

Adelle Purdham is a writer, teacher, and parent disability advocate. She holds an MFA in creative nonfiction writing and founded The Write Retreat.

PART 4

SO GOD MADE A MOTHER

strong

✕

A mother sometimes wonders if she has what it takes. Can she teach her children all they need to know? Can she conquer her own fears? Can she really let her babies go? If only she understood just how strong she's always been.

HER VIEW FROM HOME

The Lost Boy

LESLIE MEANS

×

You know that part in the movie *Home Alone* when Kevin's mom realizes she left him at home? And then she sits up in her seat in the plane and yells, "KEVIN!" to all the passengers? And then she feels like a terrible mother even though everyone convinces her it's totally normal to leave your kid at home?

I've been there. I didn't leave my son home alone, but I did lose him. And I felt like the worst mother in the history of mothers.

Let's back up.

For our daughter Grace's birthday, she invited five of her friends to watch a theater show at our local park.

We arrived, checked in, gathered all our goodies and drinks, and made our way to our reserved spot. "Follow the guys in the bright vests," we told the kids. I stood in the back of the line so we wouldn't lose a kid along the way.

You already know I failed.

We ventured to our spot on the grass and began handing out drinks.

"Who had Coke? Who had water?" and so on. But when we got to Sprite, the one person who requested Sprite—our son, Keithan—was missing.

My husband said, "Les, where's Keithan?"

I panicked. "I thought he was with the group?"

I frantically searched the crowd, but I didn't see his cute little face. Then I yelled, "Keithan!" at the same volume Kevin's mom yelled for her son.

Kyle ran up the hill to find help, and that's when a voice came over the loudspeaker. In front of hundreds of people, we heard, "We have a boy named Keithan up front with us, and he's looking for his mom, Leslie."

Our teenage daughter, Ella, ran to the stage as I funneled through the people. Keithan ran into her arms and then finally made his way into mine.

I saw tears soaking his face, and my heart shattered.

"I thought I lost my family," he said as I hugged him tighter.

"I followed the guys in the vests," he told me. But he hadn't stopped. Once we made our way to our spot in the grass, he kept following the park volunteers. And that's where he lost us.

"I'm so sorry, buddy," I told him. "We love you so much."

He was only lost for a few minutes, but those short minutes could have been devastating. I'm so thankful to all the people who helped get our sweet guy back into my arms.

And to the moms who came up to me after the incident to tell me this had happened to them too: thank you for assuring me these things happen in real life, to real people—not just to fictional characters on the big screen.

The truth is, motherhood brings with it all sorts of moments that test us and stretch us in ways we can't predict. Maybe it's a moment of panic over a child who wandered away. Maybe it's a heartbreaking diagnosis or a battle you don't feel capable of fighting. Maybe it's a random Tuesday that just feels overwhelming and long and hard.

But I've noticed something about these moments, and I bet you have too—they make us so unbelievably strong. They cause us to dig deep and fight back and never, ever give up.

You'll read some examples of that strength in the next few stories, and I think it will remind you what a fierce mama heart beats inside you too.

Mothers Are Made in the Trenches

LIZZY M. CHRISTIAN

When we see a new mother, the side we usually see is the doting mama—proud of the beautiful life she helped bring into the world.

She is proud to be called *Mom*.

Proud to be a safe place for her baby.

Proud that her ravaged body grew and birthed that little miracle.

Proud of the beautiful story unfolding before her very eyes.

She gets to be the one to see this child grow, flourish, and chase their dreams. She gets to be the one to introduce them to Jesus.

She sees their eyes light up like a Christmas tree when they become passionate about something.

She sees them make their first friend, sees them offer a hand to someone who's hurting, sees them befriend the child sitting alone in the cafeteria.

She sees them fall in love, raise a family of their own, and find their God-given passion.

She is the vessel God is using to raise this new life to be a world changer. And she takes it ever so seriously.

She studies and loves every part of her baby. She knows each intricate detail, down to the tiny freckle on the right side of their ankle or the one piece of hair that's longer than the rest.

What we don't often see is the way that mother sobs alone in the bathroom or during middle-of-the-night feedings, feeling like she's not enough.

We don't see the dark thoughts from the enemy creeping into her mind—the ones telling her she isn't enough. The ones telling her she's failing. The ones making her question her worth and her God-given abilities.

We don't see her mascara-stained face as she stands in the scalding-hot shower, disgusted at the extra flab and stretch marks across her body. She yearns to feel beautiful in her own skin again—or maybe for the very first time.

We don't see a new mom fighting physical ailments. Her heart soars with a love she's never felt before, but her body betrays her. She's weak and exhausted, as feeble as a boiled lasagna noodle, unable to find the strength to flourish. She wonders how she's going to get up again in less than two hours to comfort her crying child.

She feels distant from herself, like she's fighting a battle she knows nothing about. Her postpartum emotions are an unknown darkness. The lightning-bolt rush of fear for her baby's safety and the hurricane of emotions that overwhelm her push her soul further into a sea of perplexing, silent pain.

But the postpartum mother is strong and resilient. When she's rocking a fussy baby at 2 a.m. When she's changing a soiled diaper for the third time in an hour. When she's running on no sleep but still making sure her precious babe is fed, changed, and prayed over. When she's quietly changing her spit-up-covered shirt because the baby finally drifted off after she spent an hour pacing the dark hallway.

The postpartum mama in the trenches of motherhood is a warrior.

You are a warrior.

Every task you accomplish matters and makes a difference. Even when it feels mundane and insignificant.

Every selfless act of courage helps your child learn to soar. Every ounce of love prepares their heart for something more, something bigger, something beyond. Every small action has purpose.

Every diaper you change.

Every soiled outfit you wash.

Every pea-sized dot of diaper rash cream you apply.

Every song you sing.

Every prayer you whisper.

It all matters.

Your time in the trenches can be beautiful and miraculous, and dark and lonely. Don't be afraid to ask for help.

You aren't failing. Every task is significant. You aren't fighting this battle alone.

God called you to fulfill this beautiful mission, and He won't abandon you. Not during a midnight feed. Not when you're sobbing in the shower. Not when you're questioning your worth. Never.

You were handpicked by God to mother your beautiful child, and God wants you to flourish.

Rock that baby.

Sing that song.

Proclaim God's amazing plans for your baby.

Don't let Satan tell you what you're doing is insignificant. Your mission field might look like singing lullabies and changing diapers right now, but it's a way for you to change the world.

Lizzy M. Christian is a Fire wife, mom of three, vacuuming enthusiast, non-rhythmic dancer, iced coffee lover, and founder of the *Fire Wife Chronicles* blog.

I Wasn't Ready

EMILY GRAHAM

It didn't matter that I wasn't ready.

When the doctor said, "This baby is breech—we'll need to schedule a C-section," I felt a cavern open in my stomach. My nerves revved from zero to a hundred.

What she said next was something I never imagined: "How about five o'clock tonight?"

This motherhood thing was about to get real—fast.

It didn't matter, as I sat perched on the side of the operating room table, that I wasn't ready. I couldn't tell if my body was shaking from the cold or from fear.

When the anesthesiologist asked, "Does the needle feel like it's in the right place, in the center of your spine?" I didn't know how to respond. How was I supposed to know? If the nurse hadn't been hugging me in position, I'd surely have tried to make a run for it.

Thankfully he got it right, because soon after, I was lying on a table staring at the ceiling tiles, trying to calm my body and steady my breathing, terrified beyond words.

When they placed that baby in my arms, I honestly thought he would shake right out. I held him so tight. I couldn't believe he was here—he was real.

It didn't matter that I wasn't ready when we were discharged and sent home two days later. There was no manual in sight, no plan for how all this would go. I was sent out into the world, expected to know how to keep this baby alive. I had no clue what I was doing.

Sitting in the dark, rocking a baby every night, I had never felt so alone and unseen. Yet it was in these trenches that I became a mother.

With motherhood came a change, a shift in the way I showed up in the world.

I learned to dig deep and push past my own comfort zone. I found confidence through trial and error, knowing that everything I did, every decision I made, was with his best interest at heart. The road was bumpy at times. There were tears shed—his and mine. Yet somehow we figured it out together.

Love expanded and intensified beyond what I ever thought possible, simply because he existed. My chest swelled with pride, and an incredible energy spilled from my pores. I felt whole. I had purpose. He made me brave.

It didn't matter that I wasn't ready when he took his first steps. He giggled as his little hand pulled away from mine, so proud he no longer needed me to steady him. He toddled forward without looking back. This was just the start.

When he was a toddler, I was always chasing him, trying to keep up. The exhaustion of motherhood often felt like more than I could bear. But there was beauty. Laughter. Fun. So much fun!

It didn't matter that I wasn't ready to drop him off at his first day of school and just . . . leave. He was so bold, so excited. A big boy who no longer needed his mom by his side to help him engage with the world. He had the absolute best day while I counted down the minutes until pickup.

He soaked things up like a sponge—a little man, wise beyond his years. He made friends easily, always cheering on the underdog. It was his nature to do what he could to lift up those around him. He wanted to be sure no one was left out.

As time went on, our family grew. He loved his sisters hard. This life we'd built felt perfect. I often watched in pure wonder, taking mental snapshots.

It didn't matter that I wasn't ready when he didn't wake up.

I thought he was finally sleeping, exhausted after feeling sick. It came on so suddenly. A false sense of security took over as he was tucked into his hospital bed.

The next twenty-four hours were a total blur, yet they are permanently burned into my brain.

My precious boy, on life support. A rapid decline and numerous tests without answers. An out-of-body experience when the doctor said, "There's nothing more we can do."

For twelve hours I held him, knowing my world would never be the same, trying to imagine this life without him in it. I tried to memorize every single piece of him, because I knew I would need these visuals for whatever came next.

It didn't matter that I wasn't ready when the machine pumped his last breath. Death was already there, waiting to stake its claim.

Leaving the body of someone you love, walking out of a hospital with nothing but memories . . . it changes you.

With bereaved motherhood came destruction—in me and within my family. There is not a space untouched. We picked up the pieces as best we could, trying to rebuild around this hole that can't be filled.

I thought I'd learned to dig deep, to survive. This was another level—impossible, really. Yet somehow, time keeps moving forward.

Living slowly returns, though different from before. Laughter and joy creep back in. And impossibly, there is still so much beauty. Now there's a bittersweet entanglement of life and grief, every moment blending what is and what should be.

I've realized it doesn't matter that we aren't ready for all life has in store for us. If we just hang on, through trial and error and a little faith, we will figure it out. And we are never alone.

And though I may not be able to hold my child in my arms for now, I am still his mother and he is still making me brave.

Emily Graham is an author and grief coach at *After Child Loss*, empowering other bereaved parents with tools and support to live again after loss.

When Motherhood Looks Different from What You Planned

WHITNEY BALLARD

×

I sat in the bed of my truck holding a pregnancy test.

I thought I would cry when the second line popped up, but I just felt numb. I stared out at the field—the place I used to go with him in what seemed like a different lifetime.

I'd made a trip to the pharmacy right after school, but was too scared to take the test at home. I told myself if it was negative, I'd still go to my 5 p.m. shift at the local BBQ restaurant.

I called in sick that night.

I studied the blades of grass stuck to my bare feet as I set the test down beside me. My flip-flops lay on the ground below as my legs dangled. My chest felt so tight I thought all the oxygen had escaped my lungs. As numbness turned to anger, I felt hot all over.

I was so incredibly angry. Angry I'd have to make a decision about this pregnancy alone. Angry I'd have to tell my parents alone. Angry at myself for being so stupid. Angry at God for the terrible timing. Angry at every single person who'd taken one of these dang tests and been happy. Mostly, angry for feeling alone.

Alone. That's how I'd felt at the funeral two weeks earlier. And how I felt now, carrying his baby.

I wish there was a word like *widow* to describe the one left behind by a loved one you never got the chance to marry. I wish there was a word for a father who never got to meet his baby. I had no title, yet I wasn't ready to take on the one of *mother*.

I didn't know if I wanted kids at all, especially not at sixteen and alone.

The grass on the bottom of my feet became unbearably sticky as the tears finally started to fall. I thought how silly this was—reading a pregnancy test by myself in the middle of a field, not at all like those women in movies. I couldn't help but laugh and cry at the unfortunate events that had rewritten my life.

I wanted so desperately to tell somebody. To tell *him*. I knew this wouldn't be happy news to anyone, but if he were here, it might not be quite as devastating. I took my eyes off the ground my tears had soaked and looked up at the blue sky with the sun peeking out, far too cheerily, through clouds.

Then, right there in that field, I talked to him.

"You're going to be a daddy. I'm going to be a mom. I miss you. I wish you could have known."

There was nothing but silence.

I waited for a response I would never get as I began to sob with a nauseous stomach and a shattered heart.

He never answered, so instead I was forced to talk to God for the first time in a very long time.

"How will I do this?" I asked desperately. I was lying on my side now, letting the grooves of the truck bed dig into my ribs, not caring anymore. I thought how nice it would be to never get up. How easy it would be to end it all.

But something happened to me as I cried out to God. Beneath the fear and worry and numbness, I felt my body grow calm. It was a sudden sense of peace— the kind only God can bring.

"But, God, if I have this baby, my life will be so messed up. My path will look different from what I always imagined."

And that's okay, God reminded me.

"But I have all these plans for myself, and I had plans for us, and now he's gone. Don't take anything else from me, please."

He said, *I have plans for you too. Just wait and see.*

"But, God, I have nothing."

You have me.

That's when God made this mother. In the unlikeliest of ways. In the most uncertain of circumstances. In the very moment I hit rock bottom. He made a miracle from an absolute mess; He brought beauty from ashes.

He made a now twenty-six-year-old mother of two, wife, writer, and Christ follower from a grieving and pregnant sixteen-year-old girl.

I carried that pregnancy, had that baby, and chased my dreams—and never once was I alone.

"But I have all these plans for myself," I once pleaded.

And He so graciously told me, *I have plans for you too.*

Just wait and see.

Whitney Ballard is a teen mom turned storyteller from small-town Alabama, living life backward and writing about it along the way.

I Want to Fight
Your Battles for You—
but I Won't

BAILEY KOCH

×

My husband and I were raised by a generation that didn't discuss mental illness. Case in point: when Grandma was taken to an in-patient mental health facility after a failed suicide attempt, others were simply told she was sick and in the hospital.

"What hospital is she in, so we can send a get-well card?" people asked.

Silence. Change the subject.

As adults, we realized that silence served no positive purpose. Still, it was scary to move past what we'd always known. By the time we started contemplating opening up about our reality with severe depression, my husband had survived more than five suicide attempts. Would we be judged? We own a small business—would the truth cause customers to go elsewhere?

But silence was slowly killing us both. We felt alone. Unheard. Confused. Terrified. Something had to change. We needed to be honest, starting with our own family.

At the time, our boys were small, so we were creative with our words to help them separate their daddy from his depression: "Daddy's brain tells him to do things that could hurt him. He needs help to stay safe and get his brain healthy again so he can come home to us. He's in a special hospital where they're taking really good care of him. They're helping Daddy learn it's okay to ask for help."

We must have done something right, because our kids seem to understand how to separate the human from the mental illness better than we do. I'm still trying to comprehend it all—learning how to take care of my own mental health while my world revolves around caring for and raising others.

But I wasn't prepared for my teenager to feel like ending his life was the only option to ending his own pain.

When my teen ran to me, terrified that his brain had told him to swallow pills and end his life, I felt like I was learning how to understand mental illness right along with him. On one hand, I was proud—my son asked for help! He even used the words "My brain told me." *Thank you, Lord, that my son knows this isn't his fault.*

On the other hand, I wondered if this was something I was responsible for. *Did I cause this? How can I fix it? How can I be the strong one, the mom he needs right now, while I'm just as terrified as he is of the monster living inside his head?*

These thoughts weren't new. I'd tried to be the reason my husband was okay for years until I finally realized I couldn't be. Mental illness is bigger than I am. My husband's choice to accept help—one that's so difficult to make when the brain is clouded by negative and dark thoughts—is beyond me. I can't be the reason my husband is okay; I know this. But this was my *child*. Wasn't it my job to make him okay? Couldn't I fix him if I just tried hard enough?

But life taught me better. Mental illness is bigger than motherhood.

My child needs more help than I can give. Sometimes we have no other choice but to trust others with our child, our world.

I had a choice in that moment my son came to me. I could have felt like a failure—the mom who couldn't keep her child safe at home. Or I could have felt like the rock star I am—the mom who left my son, my world, in a youth mental-health facility because I knew he needed more help than I could provide. He needed me to do for him what I've learned to do for his father. He needed to learn how to accept help—we all did.

And sometimes fighting for your children means accepting this truth: their world is much bigger than you.

Leaving my son at the hospital was the hardest thing I've ever done. He sobbed. He begged me to take him home. I held him tighter than I had the day he came into the world, and I whispered, "Oh, my love, I'll do everything in my power to keep you safe, and this is what I have to do for you. These people know more than I do right now. They know how to help you. This is where you're safe. This is where you'll learn to understand your brain. This is where you'll learn it's okay to not be okay. I love you too much to not ask for help. It's not just you and me. It's not just you and me against the world. It's you and me and the world against mental illness—and it's time to fight. I love you."

Then I left. It was the best thing I've ever done as a mother.

When we teach our kids early how to accept help, they win, because they are so far ahead of where we were at their age. Honesty saved our child's life. Open discussion about mental health saved our child's life. Accepting help saved our child's life.

During that difficult time, my son learned how strong he is. He stayed. He talked. He prayed. He met with doctors. He learned what he could do to help himself. He healed.

And he did it all without his mother.

Bailey Koch, with her husband Jeremy, began writing at *Anchoring Hope for Mental Health* after realizing healing comes in the acceptance of help.

I Wasn't Supposed to Do This

KELLY CERVANTES

×

I never wanted to be a stay-at-home mother. Not as a child, as a young adult, or when I became a mother at the age of thirty. Financial independence was important to me, but it was more than that—I have an insufferable ambition that was not going to be fulfilled shaping a child into the best human I could possibly mold.

Yes, I enjoyed being a mother, but it just wasn't the be-all, end-all of my life. It's kind of like how some people are passionate cooks and others cook to eat—I definitely fell into the cook-to-eat kind of mom category. I loved being a mom *and* I enjoyed working. Period.

Then one evening in late May 2016, my actor-husband called to tell me he had booked the role of a lifetime: Alexander Hamilton in the smash-hit musical of the same name, opening for the first time outside New York City, in Chicago. I was out to dinner with colleagues celebrating my last day working for a company I'd been with for the last five years. The following week, I was set to begin a new job and was really excited about it.

On the train ride home that night, with adrenaline from my husband's news still coursing through my veins, I began to process what all this meant for my life. On its face, this was phenomenal news: a huge jump for my husband's career, a major financial boost for our family—but also *Hamilton*! I mean, the theater nerd in me was fangirling over my own husband.

But it wasn't that simple. It never really is.

Just three days earlier, our infant daughter had been diagnosed with epilepsy after having a seizure at daycare. Now I'd just learned we would be moving to Chicago in three months and my husband would be in the thick of rehearsals in the meantime. It dawned on me then I would have to turn down the fancy new job to care for my family, find our new home in Chicago, choose a school for our four-year-old son, and select new doctors for our newly diagnosed daughter.

As late spring turned into summer, our daughter's condition worsened, and any hope I had of picking up my career in Chicago faded. Our daughter needed me. My family needed me.

Literally overnight, I had gone from having a successful career to being a stay-at-home-mom—you know, that job I never wanted. It happened so quickly it would take months for me to process the change. When I was finally able to slow down and take in our new life, it was the dead of winter in Chicago. Boxes had been unpacked, *Hamilton* had opened to rave reviews, and everyone in my family had found their new rhythm.

Well, everyone except me.

By the end of each day, I lay in bed waiting for my husband to come home from the theater, filled with resentment for the standing ovations he got each night. Unlike when I'd exceeded sales goals and received my own congratulations, no one was handing me gold stars for managing my daughter's complicated schedule of doctor and therapy appointments in between my son's extracurricular activities while also adhering to her strict medication schedule, keeping groceries in the fridge, and ensuring there were clean clothes in the closet. I loved my family immensely, but I was depressed and unfulfilled.

It would take years of therapy, medication, and open communication with my husband before I accepted and grew to love my career change. I still struggle with my lack of financial contribution to our family, but I realize no price can be placed on my value.

I was able to find additional fulfillment in volunteer work with CURE

Epilepsy, a nonprofit dedicated to funding epilepsy research, and in sharing our journey with other families on similar paths via my blog and social media.

I know now the rug can be pulled out from underneath you in the blink of an eye, and when that happens, it's irrational to expect to land on your feet. It can take years to pull yourself back up to standing, but the legs beneath you will be stronger than before. And the position you find yourself in may be more rewarding than you ever could have imagined.

Kelly Cervantes is an award-winning writer, speaker, and advocate best known for her blog, *Inchstones*. Her debut book, *Normal Broken*, releases fall 2023.

Reaching for God in the Dark

JASMINE CHATMAN

✕

The day I saw that glow in my baby's eye will be forever etched in my brain. I knew something wasn't right, and I needed someone to listen. How we ended up at St. Jude Children's Research Hospital is nothing short of a miracle.

After a series of tests, my then eighteen-month-old daughter, Sariyah, was diagnosed with retinoblastoma. My husband and I were pulled away from our four other children as we spent a month six hours from home with our baby. Eventually we were able to come home between treatments, but those eleven treatments were heart shattering, to say the least.

After the dust settled, I realized I'd been in survival mode the entire time. Those gut-wrenching hours in the medicine room. The chemo, cryotherapy, and laser therapy in her eye, which caused it to swell so much it looked like it would burst. The pokes, prods, and screams; the separation from my family; and the crippling anxiety.

We did an end-of-chemo celebration for her even though I was still weighed down with fear. I felt like I was just going through the motions. Coming out of that fog was like learning to live all over again.

One day I caught a glimpse of myself in the bathroom mirror. I gasped. I didn't even recognize myself. Sweat was pouring down my temples, my under-eyes were dark and swollen from a lack of sleep, and my hair was disheveled and tangled. I was holding tightly to a cleaning rag, trying to believe I had some semblance of control.

I imagine the whole time God was gently nudging me to let go and hand it all over to Him. That's when I knew I needed more help.

Therapy was a start, but nothing could have prepared me for what came next: Sariyah's cancer was back. Her doctor started talking about scheduling plaque radiotherapy. It felt like all the blood was rushing to my head, and I could hardly see straight. She had already gone through so much, and now this?

When the recovery room called for me after her next surgery, I was reminded of the evil lurking just beneath the surface. Her right eye was already swollen shut. I stood by her side until she woke up, agitated and disoriented. I held her close, entangled in monitor cords and her blanket.

I was the last person she saw before she drifted off and the first person she saw when she woke up. What a juxtaposition of feelings—privileged, grateful, and heartbroken, all at once.

After she was cleared to leave, I carefully buckled her in the stroller and we made our way to the hotel as fast as we could.

My knees hit the floor, and there in the hotel room, my heart broke all over again. I pleaded with God until I could barely catch my breath. I was upset with cancer, angry that it could brazenly return like this.

Before my mind could process what my body was doing, I walked over to the window. I needed to feel the sunlight on my skin. No matter how dark things seemed, the light always finds a way in. I took note of the way the rays of light fell on my daughter, sound asleep in her stroller. I was overwhelmed by a sense of peace so profound it took my breath away.

The radiation ended up causing a cataract so severe the doctor could no longer see in the back of her eye, so she needed cataract surgery. Now, many months out from her initial diagnosis, each follow-up visit feels like another storm. I still wake up covered in sweat, shaken by another nightmare, reaching in the dark for the Bible on my nightstand.

It's really God I'm reaching for. I'm the woman in the book of Matthew, audaciously reaching for the hem of His garment. As I grapple with the tension between sorrow and joy again, I'm slowly learning the dance. But I'm growing and healing with each step.

We all end up thrown in the ring at some point, wrestling with something we didn't expect. Some blows hit so hard they leave us scarred and broken. Even so, our opponent is no match for God, who is undefeated every time. He never leaves our side, and we never have to fight alone.

Keep reaching for God in the dark—He is our Light.

Jasmine Chatman is a mother of five, including a tiny cancer warrior. She hopes to inspire others to pursue passion and purpose in trials and pain.

Beyond the Picket Fence

CELESTE YVONNE

✕

When we took our three-year-old to the pediatrician, the doctor didn't have the answers I was seeking.

"Behavioral problems are normal at this age, but the elevated levels you indicate may need to be explored further. For now, there's not much you can do. Come back in a few years and we can do some testing if it's still a problem."

A few years? I couldn't even get through a day without a full-blown panic attack every time the phone rang, my heart stopping if I saw the daycare's number.

I was terrified, heartbroken, and confused. My son's school made it clear they couldn't put up with any more of his aggressive behavior. My husband and I were at wit's end trying to manage the power struggles, and while our youngest child was still just a baby, we worried for both our children as our oldest's erratic, impulsive behavior only seemed to be getting worse.

"Please," I practically begged, "is there anything we can do now?"

The doctor paused, and as if reading straight into my soul, then said, "Your son will need a positive, stable, controlled environment to thrive."

And just like that, things clicked into place. I understood the assignment.

You see, while we looked like a happy-go-lucky family on the outside, there were darker forces at play. I was drinking about a bottle of wine a night, often alone and in secret. Just a few months earlier, I'd written a prayer request at church, saying, "I am sabotaging everything good in my life."

My drinking wasn't a visible problem yet—but undoubtedly it would become one. And my son was bearing the brunt of my internal chaos.

The hitting, the impulsivity, and the tantrums that could last for hours? We didn't know the cause, and we wouldn't be able to put a label on it for another three years. But his environment could be vastly improved. And it had to start with me.

When people ask me what made me quit drinking, I ask them how much time they have. There were signs my drinking was coming to an end long before I put down the bottle. The voice, starting as a whisper and ending with screams and sobs, finally burrowed into my head and heart on a cold, somber Monday morning in December.

It's hard to describe emotional rock bottom, other than to say my worst nightmare was laid out before me like a bed of nails. *Is this what you want?* God called to me. *Because this is the direction you're going.*

I saw my father, an alcoholic my whole life. I saw him choosing alcohol over his own family. I saw a massive stroke, a life in pieces, and a family broken by addiction.

No, God, this is not what I want. I want family. I want happiness. I want children who know what to expect when they come home every day.

My son was eventually diagnosed with ADHD and autism spectrum disorder. But the biggest change in our family's dynamic and health didn't come from a diagnosis, a new school, or therapy. It came that day in the pediatrician's office, when I recognized the biggest assignment—the real opportunity—was for me to get my act together and be the parent my kids need.

Celeste Yvonne is five years sober and an advocate for mothers who struggle with addiction, which she refers to as *The Ultimate Mom Challenge.*

The Little
Left-Behinds

ASHLI BREHM

×

When I was growing up, my sister and I shared a bedroom. It was the eighties, so this was not the "we shared a suite" era. Our room had a normal closet, not a sprawling, Pinterest-worthy walk-in. And in that small, square room, there was not a themed kid-a-palooza; it was just the necessities. A dresser. A desk. A set of solid wood bunk beds.

The two of us got along easily, which I credit to her personality. As the middle child of our family, she was laid back and easygoing. As the youngest, I was all over the place—and my housekeeping skills reflected as much.

Every so often, my mom would throw her hands in the air and declare this sister of mine and I would not be leaving our room until everything was in its proper place. It was time for us to clean our room. Like *really* clean our room, not just "kid clean" it.

We would clean and clean, and eventually we'd have about twenty-four random items scattered on the carpet. Maybe a shoe for a Barbie. A piece of paper we wanted to keep. The part to a toy that was long gone. Other miscellaneous junk.

We'd both walk around aimlessly, looking at the scraps, not sure what to do next. We knew all the pieces needed to be picked up, but we didn't know where they should go. By that point, we'd been looking at the mess for too long. We just needed water. And bread. And civilization beyond our bedroom jail.

Okay. A *little* dramatic, I know. But when we got to that point, we just kind of felt stuck.

Eventually, I'm sure my sister completed the task for both of us. Or my mom secretly tossed the last reminders of our overwhelming mess. All I know for sure is that I got to a point when I knew I was too in it to get out by myself.

Now, as a mom, I find myself in my mother's shoes, throwing my hands in the air and declaring a day for the whole crew to clean. Pick up their rooms, closets, and yes, even under the beds. (The underbeds in our house are like secret burial grounds. I have found myself lifting the quilt to locate a shoe or rescue a library book, terrified that something from *Stranger Things* is going to nibble off my arm.) It's a situation—the clearing of clutter in the spaces they see as their very own.

On the days when the big clean commences, it's a daunting undertaking. At some point, the troops get owly. They begin to grow weary and woeful. And I know when those moans and groans gather, they are down to the bits. The twenty-four random things in the middle of the floor—things that belong in the trash can, but my kids can't stand to think of parting with. They view these items as personal artifacts they couldn't possibly live without, like ripped-up construction paper, a gum container, and a packet of Stevia.

When that happens, the mom in me knows I should stick to my guns and make them finish the job they started. But several years ago, when these young men we get to call ours were six, four, and two, I was diagnosed with breast cancer. And while I now get to live a gorgeous after-cancer reality, that experience has impacted the way I see those last twenty-four things on the floor.

So I often do what we as parents are never supposed to do. As long as they aren't being whiny jerks, I tell them to be done. I release them from cleaning duty and send them back out into their world. Sometimes, in a move that would have made me lose my ever-loving mind before cancer happened to us, we leave the left-behinds overnight while we sleep and refresh. Other times I gather up the leftovers and throw them in the "keepsake bin" (aka the trash can), and they never ask where it all went.

Sometimes we just do what we can do.

There are just parts of life like that. We go through something hard—something that's an utter and unwound mess—and we keep our composure . . . for a while. But at some point, it becomes too much. We've been doing it too long. We've been sitting in it too long, looking at it too long. And when we see the random bits we're meant to figure out a place for, none of them make sense to us anymore. And even though we know those pieces aren't meant to fit with us anymore, we can't just let them go or get rid of them or ignore them or cope with them. We just can't.

And that's when we need help. We need a rope thrown to help us out of the muck we've gotten mired in. We don't dare ask for it, though, because everyone's got their own mess to sort through.

But guess what? We aren't meant to do this alone. So if help shows up—even if we can't ask for it—we can absolutely accept it. Because sometimes we just need someone to offer us hope. To be our glimmer of goodness.

Whether it's cleaning up after ourselves or something bigger, we all have moments we struggle to pick up the pieces and put them in the right spot. Eventually, a fresh start on a fresh day allows for a fresh perspective, and we see how things look better by morning light. Then we can see the things that really matter and get rid of ones that don't deserve our stress. And it starts to feel like less of a mess.

So when you feel like you just don't know how you'll make it all work, remember *you* don't have to, because we were made to live in community. And be loved there. Gum wrappers and all.

Ashli Brehm loves being alive. She also really loves her husband and three boys. Writing and chemo saved her life. And she thinks God rocks.

Grief Is like Crocs

SHELBY SKILES

×

I have very tiny feet—as in, I'm thirty-three and can comfortably wear a women's size 5½ or 6. It's sometimes frustrating to find shoes because stores usually order only a few boxes in those sizes, so once they're gone, they're really gone. I also struggle to find shoes without some cartoon character on them.

My daughter, Sophie, also had tiny feet. Her favorite shoes were her navy Crocs. Whenever we left the house, she had to be wearing the Crocs. Regardless of how much I urged her to put on cuter shoes, she brought her beloved foam clogs to me every time.

She loved them so much that when she died at two-and-a-half years old, we buried her in them. Well, we buried her in a new pair of navy Crocs, because I kept her beloved, well-worn pair for myself.

I've decided grief is like Crocs.

Crocs are ugly. They feel weird and uncomfortable when you first put them on, because they have those bumps on the inside and you inevitably get a blister from that rubber strap across the back of your heel. It's true that they come in all kinds of colors and designs, but no matter what you do to them, they're still ugly. Even if you attach the cute little characters to the top holes, they still aren't that appealing. Yet you wear them, and over time, they sort of grow on you.

Grief is the same way. It's uncomfortable and ugly when you first put it on. It's full of bumps and will form a blister that makes you limp. No matter what your grief looks like or what you do with it, it's still ugly. You can cry, rage, stay busy, or lie in bed for days . . . it's all ugly. Yet you keep wearing it, and the Lord wears it with you. He feels the blisters. He is the bandage that will soothe the raw skin.

If given the choice, I'd exchange grief in a heartbeat for something more comfortable. Nevertheless, after you've worn grief for a while, you start to break it in. You find that over time you can bear the bumps, and your skin is a little thicker so blisters don't form as easily. You still don't really like it and you still think it's ugly, but you gain a grudging kind of appreciation.

No one chooses the life of a grieving parent. God never wanted that as part of our lives. Death wasn't supposed to be in the picture. But when the world broke long ago, our Father took on the role of the ultimate grieving Parent. In doing so, He can help us in our grief, and He promises us an eternity with Him and our lost children.

He comes alongside us in our ugly grief and our raw hurt—and He helps us break in the Crocs.

Shelby Skiles started *Sophie the Brave* to chronicle her daughter's cancer journey and continues to write about how her daughter's death and grief still impact her life.

The Gospel of
the Bathroom Floor

LIZ PETRONE

✕

My son, Luca, was born into my husband's arms on the floor of our en suite bath-room. We didn't plan it that way, but that's how it happened. When my mortal time is up on this earth and the highlight reel of my life flashes before my eyes, that memory will no doubt be there. The way my husband laid him so gently on my chest. The way our three older children stood outside the bathroom door while everything went down, their ears pressed against the wood. How, from where I lay spent on the cool tile, I could see the shadow of their feet under the door as they danced in excitement.

The truth is, I was no stranger to that bathroom floor. I'd found myself there before—not in labor, but in hiding, in frustration, and eventually, in mourning. A house full of children brings with it many blessings, but privacy isn't one of them, and a bathroom with a door that locks has a way of becoming a mother's space of her own for stolen moments of quiet desperation.

I'd lost my own mother three weeks before that bathroom birth. Or rather, I lost her in bits and pieces for a decade or two before that, watching as she was carried out of our lives by an unrelenting current of mental illness and substance abuse. Then I lost the rest of her to suicide when I was thirty-seven weeks pregnant—much too big to gracefully fall to the bathroom floor, but unable to stop myself from the learned habit of taking my pain there to sort through in peace.

I thought I'd prepared for both of these things—the biggest things—birth and death. When I found out I was pregnant for what I knew was the last time, I wrote a birth plan and made a playlist and hired a photographer and found the perfect midwife. I did prenatal yoga and visualized all the ways I wanted this birth to go. But then we, too, were swept up in that unrelenting current and carried to a new place—a place I didn't recognize from my visions, a place where my mother was dead.

I thought I'd prepared for that too—as if you could, as if that's even a thing. But loving someone while losing them is like that. You grasp at things you think you might be able to control, the ways you might be able to protect yourself. So I tried to set boundaries and make walls and fence myself in, but none of it mattered in the end, because she was still my mother. And then she was gone.

And so I locked myself in the bathroom to weep or wail or just breathe for a minute before I could reemerge into my life, make snacks, tuck babies into bed, keep going.

When I look back on Luca's birth now, I can't exactly remember if I went into the bathroom to mourn or to labor that time, and I suppose in the end it doesn't matter, because the line between the two is blurry anyway. There is death and there is birth and there is loss and there is life, and there are stolen moments of deep pain on the bathroom floor in all of it. What I do remember is how when Luca was born, his eyes were the same striking shade of deep blue my mother's had been, and how when we opened the door to the dancing feet on the other side, light spilled into the room right alongside our children.

It's been years since I lost my mother, years since Luca was born, but I still visit the peace of the bathroom floor when I need to, when life is too loud or too hard or too much. I still find solace in the click of the lock and the coolness of the tile. But something shifted there that day, and I don't find myself on the bathroom floor seeking solitude anymore. Instead, I find myself listening in the quiet under my own breath for the memory of that day, for the patter of dancing feet by the door. And sometimes, if I'm very quiet, for the whisper of my mother underneath it all.

Liz Petrone is the author of *The Price of Admission: Embracing a Life of Grief and Joy.*

PART 5

SO GOD MADE A MOTHER
feel like home

"I am where
my children fit—
forever, for always,
for anything."

JENNIFER VAIL

The Kitchen

LESLIE MEANS

×

I cried when she sent me the photo. "The kitchen is cleaned out. Demo starts tomorrow," she wrote. It wasn't one of those simple cries. It was an ugly cry, the kind that squishes your face, turns your cheeks red, and makes your nose run. The kind of cry that makes you wonder, in the moment, if there are enough tissues in the world to absorb your tears.

Then she added, "I'm surprised how emotional this makes me."

Me too.

My sister Lindsay texted the photo. It was the old kitchen in the house where we grew up. My great-grandpa moved into that farmhouse in 1901. My grandpa grew up there, then my dad. I grew up there too, along with my three older sisters.

A few years ago, Mom and Dad built a new house down the road, beyond the pasture, and my sister and her husband moved in to the farmhouse. It's my favorite place in the entire world, and I pray I'll never have to see it leave our family.

But back to that kitchen.

For a few years, my sister and her family have been moving walls and changing paint colors and fixing the foundation and adding their own touches, and it looks gorgeous. The kitchen was one of the last rooms to change.

"It's going to be beautiful," I texted, "but this is making me bawl."

If I showed you the photo, here's what you would see: pink floral linoleum with chunks out of the corners. A few cupboards without handles. Dark brown cabinets that went out of style in 1992. Laminate countertops with stains. And a rotting floor under the sink.

But when my sister and I see it, it looks so much different. We see stains on the counter where we spent hours making Christmas cookies and helping Mom bake cakes. We picture our favorite Garfield cups that lived in the cabinet without the handles. Mom made us scrub those pink flowers on the floor with a toothbrush to get it clean. And we know why the floor was rotting—because those darn pipes froze each winter, causing water to leak.

It was my favorite room in the entire house. It was the place we ate Sunday dinners as a family. The place my soon-to-be husband sat down with my dad to ask for my hand in marriage. The room every big announcement and every small argument and everything in between happened. It was the heart of the home.

But the kitchen was so small, my sister and her family decided to move it to a different area of the home.

"The old kitchen space will be an office," Linds told me. It's the perfect spot for an office.

This was the final goodbye. The walls are still there, of course, and for that, I'm thankful. I know so many farm families aren't as lucky.

I'm not sure why I cried those tears, but I think it's a combination of reasons. For one thing, this is another goodbye to a childhood I loved. The goodbyes are happening more often these days as I inch closer to midlife. I cried out of gratitude for the love and comfort I felt in that space. I shed tears of thankfulness that my sister and her family now get to make it their own.

It's been a few weeks since the demolition began. The new kitchen looks like it stepped right out of a magazine. Linds sent my sisters and me a photo last week.

"What do you think this says?" she asked us. The photo showed writing on an old brick chimney, the one she uncovered and preserved. The one that sat in our kitchen but was hidden behind a wall.

"Harold and Howard," we decided.

Maybe the scrawls were measurements from my grandpa Harold and his brother when they were kids. Today they remind me that love made this house a home. It didn't begin with me, and it won't end with me, either.

That feeling of home, the one that weaves its way through generations of mothers and fathers and daughters and sons? It's the heartbeat of a family. It's safety and security and happiness and tears and love—so much love. It's what I hope you'll recognize in your own heart as you read these stories.

Did I Love You Enough?

LORI E. ANGIEL

✕

Did I do enough? I've asked myself this so many times since you were born.

Did I hold you enough, or did I let the dishes get in the way?

Did I play enough, or did I worry too much about the laundry?

Did I laugh enough? Did you see how much you filled my heart and made me smile? Or did I look too worn out or too tired?

Did I answer enough of your never-ending questions, or did I get preoccupied with dirty floors and picking up toys?

Should we have done more? More playing, more baking, more reading, more puzzles, more messes . . . or was I too busy doing *all the things*?

What did I miss? What moments did I give away cleaning a house that didn't appreciate it? I can't help but wonder.

Did you notice when I was distracted, checking email, doing work, worrying about my to-do list?

Did you feel my love, or did it feel like worry? I think of this so often.

Did my love feel heavy to you? All the corrections, trying to teach you all the time—was it bothersome? All my running after you, keeping you from harm—was it a burden?

I feel like I've been running after you for all your years. And now I feel as though I'm in a race against time.

These days I watch you leave more and more. Leaving for school. Leaving for practice. Leaving to spend time with your friends.

Leaving me behind.

Is this how it felt when I left you? When you asked me how long I'd be gone, if you could have one more hug?

If so, I'm sorry. I didn't know. "How long will you be gone?" I ask now. I would like another hug now too.

You used to wait up for me. And now I wait up for you.

I wait to see your face when you come in. I wonder if you want to talk, if you want to tell me about your day, if you want to share your burdens. If you want to tell me anything at all.

I'm still trying to keep you from harm.

I wish it all came easier for me, this process of letting you go. I keep thinking how I'm just not done. I have so much more to do. More places I want to take you, more things I want to teach you, so many things to tell you. There's more time I want to spend with you.

The years have gone so fast.

I hope you remember the hours we spent in the backyard searching for bugs and chasing butterflies. I hope you remember the days at the beach, the countless trips to the park, the walks through museums. I hope you remember I always gave you five more minutes and I pushed you as high as I could. I hope you remember summer nights with long walks and ice cream.

I hope you remember family game nights and movie nights with popcorn and treats. I hope you remember snuggles and stories before bed. I hope our road trips and vacations have left you with happy memories.

I hope you see how proud I've been watching you from the sidelines—you have no bigger fan than me. The weekend tournaments, the driving across town for practices, the rushing to games—I didn't mind. I knew this day would come. So even when it was hard, even when it was harried, it was okay with me. It was easier than watching you pull out of the driveway without me. How much I will miss watching you play.

I hope you know all I've ever wanted was to be your mom. But I didn't know how hard it would be or how much I would worry. I thought I was so strong. And right now, strength means letting you go.

I hope you know you are ready. You are everything I could have hoped for and so much more than I could have expected.

And we both can be sure my love will go with you always.

Lori E. Angiel is a loving wife, emotional mother, and *Her View From Home* contributor. She lives in western New York with her family. Go Bills!

Braiding My Own Umbilical Cord

KIRSTYN WEGNER

✕

I have never been bound to my daughter by tissue or blood.

I didn't know her before her arrival, as birth mothers instinctively do. She was never a flutter in my belly or a second heartbeat in my womb. There was no immediate intimacy between us the way there is when a newborn is placed on her biological mother's chest for the first time. There was only awkward silence and discomfort.

My daughter entered my life as a seven-year-old stranger. We were her second foster home in less than two weeks, and she was desperate for her life to return to normal. She did everything in her small power to fight this foster placement. She kicked. She screamed. She raged. She cried. She wet her pants. She refused to speak. She refused to eat. She spat her medication into the toilet. She did everything she could think of to make things hard for us in the hope that we would send her back, as though it were as simple as returning a defective waffle maker to the store.

She refused to settle into our home.

I endured her behaviors with a sort of helpless patience, knowing the only thing she wanted was not to be with me. But I was determined to love her. In fact, her resistance only made my determination stronger. Biological connection or not, my maternal instinct was strong, and I could not give up on her.

I knew the thing she needed more than anything else was to simply be held. So I offered her my arms, and she collapsed into them.

She was ten when we finalized her adoption.

As an adoptive mother, I have had to braid my own umbilical cord.

The connection we now share is the result of hard work and commitment. I had to learn to bond with her in ways that were stronger than those flimsy courthouse documents. I had to earn her trust, which was no small feat. The circumstances surrounding her adoption left her with a fractured sense of trust, so this process has been slow and challenging.

Trust is made of consistency, and consistency is made of individual moments, so I've seized every opportunity to spin threads of connection between us: nature walks and picnics, baking days and movie nights. I've braided these threads with whatever scraps I can find—a common interest, a television show, a favorite food, even math homework—and laced them with strands of stability and hope, of patience and acceptance.

This is how I've created the umbilical cord that ties me to my child. Our bond is beautiful yet tenuous, as fragile and strong and miraculous as spider-spun silk.

Sometimes this makeshift cord feels so strong she seems to have been born of my own body. When she lays her head on my chest, when she slips her hand into mine, I feel the connection we share in a visceral way, as certain as shared flesh. She is, beyond all doubt, my child.

Other times I'm acutely aware of our differences, and this cord feels so very weak. I know my daughter better than anyone else, but there are parts of her she will never give away. She's a teenager now, and she has questions about her past I can't answer. She has anger. She has pain. Despite my best efforts, I can't understand what she has been through. When she shuts me out, when she pushes me away, I feel the snap of that delicate cord breaking, and suddenly I'm adrift without her.

But no matter what happens, I can't let her go.

I'm always reaching for her, grasping at the severed strands, so I can start braiding us back together. This bond is resilient, but I must continually pick up the threads and weave them together. This is what makes us family—my choice to return to her, to connect with her, to braid my heart to hers.

This cord between us is miraculous, and my child is not the only one who is nourished by it. I, too, am fed by the moments we share, the trust I've earned, the love she returns—all made sweeter by the knowledge that our love is made of choices, not biology.

There's no obligation that joins us; there's only love.

I have chosen her, and she has chosen me, and that tether between us is nothing short of miraculous.

Kirstyn Wegner lives in rural Minnesota with her husband, daughter, stray cats, and a revolving cast of foster children. Her blog is *The Frustrated Epileptic.*

How She
Made Me Feel

JESSICA URLICHS

×

I lived in a small house growing up, but I don't remember it that way. The trees outside were as tall as could be, and the sound of pots and pans in the kitchen was large.

We didn't have a lot of money. Our car heater only started to kick in by the time we got to school. But on the weekends when the snow would fall, we'd all go outside together in our retro-colored snowsuits and catch snowflakes on our tongues.

I remember my parents throwing parties and how laughter spilled down the hallway, muffled by my bedroom door. And how only moments before I'd entertained them all with some dance routine I'd made up.

I remember my mother's smile, how she laughed and tossed her head back. It always made me happy.

I remember when I was sick how safe I felt knowing she was there, how she would hold me and be my very own blanket. How her touch was magic, because when you're young, you believe in magic, until somewhere along the way it fades, and then you become a mother yourself.

I remember the wallpaper half-peeled from the walls, waiting to be renovated. Then when I was older, we tore it down together. Music was playing, and Mom and I danced around the kitchen, stripping wallpaper as if it were ribbons of confetti.

I remember the kitchen filling with smoke one night, a furious smell wafting from the oven as Mom's hand tried to beat it away. How she bundled us into the car and we got takeout. We pulled up beside a beach somewhere and ate burgers and chips. It was silent apart from the sound of munching, but the excitement of something new and different buzzed in the air.

I remember how for every concert, she was there. For every sports event, everything that mattered to me, she was there.

I wasn't aware of the tears or the mess around me—in the house or in her life. I didn't know about the impending divorce and what it meant to her when she had to move out of the renovated house, the one she'd dreamed of, the one I always felt in my heart we fixed together.

Then it was just Mom, my two brothers, and me in a rented home with green carpet and pink walls. She worked a lot more, and we had nannies she couldn't afford. She was tired, but she still smiled. Whatever time she did have, she spent with us.

Now that I'm a mother, I sometimes wonder how Mom did it. I wonder if things wouldn't have been so hard if it weren't for us kids, if maybe her dreams would have come true, if she would have smiled more.

I wondered if she struggled because we were thriving.

Things weren't perfect, but we were never short on love, and now that I'm a mother, I try to remind myself of these things. On the days I feel like I'm sinking, like I'm getting nothing done, I look at my two greatest achievements right in front of me.

On a winter day not long ago, it was freezing outside, the walls were closing in, and both children were hanging on to my leg. The dishes were piled up, and the laundry lay scattered. I was about to put my head in my hands, when through the window, I saw snowflakes begin to dance in the air.

It was never about what we had growing up. It was never about the checklists she ticked off. It was about how she made us feel.

I smiled because I realized she was happy—maybe not always, but she was happy.

Just as I am now.

"Come on kids," I said with a smile. "Put your gloves on. Let's go outside and catch some snowflakes."

Jessica Urlichs is a poet and author who lives in New Zealand. Her honest words on motherhood have been featured worldwide.

The Mom Imposter

ANGELA ANAGNOST-REPKE

×

I allowed myself to go into my old bedroom in my parents' house—alone—and cry on the bed. My mother had been diagnosed with advanced cancer twenty-four hours earlier, and I'd just put my six-week-old daughter to sleep. Fear erupted inside me.

The bed was my island, and I wanted no one else on it. I let the tears capture me as I emptied myself onto the desolate island.

My mother crept through the doorway and slid onto the bed next to me. We faced each other, both on our sides, knees bent in. I inhaled her subtle perfume, the same kind she'd worn since I was kid. She held my hand. Her hands were soft, and her retired piano fingers were sleek. I never wanted her to leave me. The only person I wanted sympathy from was my mother, the woman with cancer. Our dark, oval eyes were glued together.

"If I die," she said, "you will be okay."

Death. She finally said it. That word had been there all day, hovering like a seagull. She began to tell me, for the hundredth time, that she lost her mother when she was just twenty-four years old and had a newborn herself. She claimed she even flourished.

"When your brother was born, he gave me life. Your kids will give *you* life too," she said.

Only I didn't want to listen to any of it, because I didn't want to envision my life without her in it.

Fidgeting with my bun, I pleaded, "You'll be there when they graduate high school."

I would not accept that my mother might die. That she could, in fact, leave me here with these two small children I was too scared to raise without her.

Without my mom, I would lose all my abilities to mother. If I could no longer call her three times every day, prompting her for her motherly "I've had four kids" wisdom, then all would be unveiled: *I don't really have what it takes. I have no idea what I'm doing on an hour-to-hour basis when it comes to my children.*

I must have been born missing something biologically. I'm not the tender type—it must have been a gene my mother failed to award to me. Yes, I loved all the baby firsts: the first smile, the first time rolling over, the first foods, the first real belly laugh. When my oldest was a baby, the sound of his cooing in his crib felt like the lyrics to my favorite song. All of it was magic, and it took my breath away. And yet I didn't want an infant attached to my breast all day. I felt like I needed more breaks than most moms.

When my son was born, I had to coax myself into softening. Daily, I practiced being selfless—that's all motherhood seems to be sometimes. I tried to balance gentleness and toughness on one of those double apothecary scales, but being hard always seemed to weigh more. If my mom died, what would come of my armor? Would it engulf me, making me all hard?

Or would my armor be completely gone? I feared any protection I had would be buried with my mother, and my vulnerabilities would be exposed for all to see. I wouldn't be able to figure out any of this motherhood stuff on my own. This is what frightened me most: that I was a fake. Without my mom, I would be a mom imposter.

Seven years later, my mother is still here. My daughter, now seven, has her grandmother's strong will. And my mom has been able to use her retired piano fingers to teach her granddaughter a few chords on the piano she handed down to her.

I almost lost my mom. Between countless chemotherapies and radiation that made her lose far too much weight, it was almost too much for her frail body. But somewhere along the way, I've dropped my armor. Now softness bleeds out of me.

It didn't happen overnight. While my mom was suffering, I was busy playing the martyr—doing everything for everyone, with my valiant spear in my hand. It wasn't until after my mom survived that I grew soft. I realized the true me was just doing the best I could. And that it was okay to fail, to drop the ball, to end up in your husband's arms sobbing because some days are just so overwhelming.

Now I know I'm not a mom imposter. I'm a mom who isn't shiny and perfect. I'm a mom who's human.

Today I'm trying to teach my kids to get themselves off any isolated islands they strand themselves on. Because islands are lonely. Instead, we're better off surrounding ourselves with people who are willing to help us, people who embrace the real us, flaws and all.

So let yourself crumble into someone else's arms. No one needs you to be a hero. Be a hero to yourself by letting others in—then you won't be any kind of imposter at all.

Angela Anagnost-Repke is a writer and educator dedicated to raising two empathetic children. She can often be found along the shores and amid the trees of northern Michigan.

I Am Where
My Children Fit

JENNIFER VAIL

✕

No matter their age, size, or issue, I am where my children fit. I am their comfort object, equal parts Mom and blanket. I am acceptance, encouragement, and safety. When the world offers only a round hole, I am where my square peg finds just the right spot. Whenever heartache is too much to bear, I am where the burden is shared.

I am where my daughter fits, soft and real, when media and magazines threaten her sense of worth. In my arms, she can hear the beat of my heart louder than the voices on the Internet. Cuddled against my shoulder, she doesn't have to worry about how much she talks or how much she cries. She can be as smart as she needs to be without worrying she'll be perceived as bossy; she can be as carefree as she wants to be without being called names; she can feel every emotion she needs to feel without being dismissed as dramatic, hormonal, or flighty.

The place in me where my daughter fits has no scales, no mirrors, and no cliques. She can talk about bugs or boys or anime or unicorns and share her hopes and dreams and wishes. My daughter will one day be a woman, and here, in the safety of our bond, I can give her advice and encourage her, teach her how to dismiss the things that don't matter and won't matter, and lovingly instruct her in the things that someday will. Cloaked within the safety of her mother is where my daughter will become her fiercest and her strongest, where she will be made ready to conquer the world.

I am where my son fits. He's the one you'll find on the outskirts, beyond the edges of what society calls "normal." There's not a place for him out there, not yet. Schools weren't built for him. Other kids don't understand him. He's an outlier and, as with many like him, he knows it. Sometimes he's okay with that; other times he can't help but feel lonely. A world built for the masses is a world that excludes my son, but I am his mother, and for now, I am right where he fits.

I understand him like no one else can. I see how his quirks are gifts; I see the beauty in the way he's made. I see the hand of God perfecting a masterpiece that other people aren't quite ready to appreciate. I have space for his ideas, his words, his big feelings, and his bigger fears. I get him, and best of all, he knows it. When others discourage him and say there's no place for him, he knows the truth: I am where he fits. I am where he is accepted, loved, heard, and understood. I am where he has an advocate. I am where he has a friend. I am all he needs me to be until the world is ready for him to be what they've missed.

I feared the day when my son would grow taller than me, worried he'd out-grow my place for him and his need for me. How could I be a safe place for him to melt into when he towered over me, when he couldn't lay his cheek against my heartbeat and feel protected, shielded, and safe in my arms? What good am I to a child when I can no longer be a physical shelter from a world that's even bigger?

He towers over me now, my son. We had to practice how to hug, which ways to wrap our arms around, over, and through each other. I can no longer scoop him up, swaddle him, or fold myself around him to shield him from the world. Now I rest my head against his chest. I hear his heartbeat and breathe in his cologne, quite different from the smell of a hospital blanket or tear-free shampoo. He's not quite ready to be a man—I'm not ready for him to be a man—and even though we had to rearrange some limbs, I am still where he fits.

I am still where he finds safety and comfort, but now I also offer dating advice and homework help. I am still where he leans while he's watching a movie on the couch, but now I offer college tips and spiritual guidance too.

We've moved from me being his world to him entering the world, from him connecting to my heartbeat to me connecting to his. Now I rest my head against his chest, a space that cradles me, a place where I will fit from now on. I squeeze the more than six feet of him and do my best to make him small inside my arms, but because he's always had a place to fit, he's learned he doesn't need to be small to be safe. Because he's had a safe place with me, he's grown confident in his place, his abilities, his size. He has grown to be able to handle more without me, and someday he'll reach a point when he won't really need me. As bittersweet as that sounds (and believe me, the words sting), I know my space for him will never go away. Better still, he knows it too.

I am where my children fit—forever, for always, for anything. Even if things shift until I am the one fitting into their lives, into their schedules, into the dent of their chests as I lay my cheek against them, I know we will always be just right for each other.

Jennifer Vail, wife, advocate, insomniac, and hip-hop enthusiast, shares passionate empathy for the atypical at *This Undeserved Life* and moms hard in her "minivanborghini."

Home Is Wherever
I'm with You

ESTEPHANIE PHELPS

×

Whenever I thought about creating a family of my own one day, I always pictured living in a house.

A house where we could run through the different rooms, just because we could. A house with a backyard where we could have a little garden (even though I am terrible at taking care of plants) and possibly a pool for hot summer days.

What we have now is not what I'd planned for or pictured. In fact, it seems quite the opposite.

Our home is a one-bedroom apartment. It's all we can give to you at the moment. We weren't able to give you a nursery, and we don't have a lot of closet space. The only bathroom we have is in the bedroom, so sometimes I have to hold it while you're sleeping. At times I try to leave the dishes alone, but the cramped counters and small sink can only hold so much.

But I've realized a home is more than these walls, more than the place we come back to at the end of the day. And while we may not have a house, we do have a home.

It's small, yes, but big things happen here. It's where I heard your laugh for the first time. It's where you said your first words. It's where we came back to after learning the doctor had some concerns about your development. It's where we continue to see your strength and what you've overcome.

It's also where I'm learning to take better care of myself, because taking the best care of you means taking care of me, too. It's where I'm learning how to conquer my fears and anxiety. It's where your father and I are learning how to communicate with each other better. Being here is teaching us so many things.

Living in a one-bedroom apartment without a backyard has allowed us to explore more places, and together we've discovered parks, creeks, lakes, and greenways. We've had the opportunity to let go of the things we didn't need and put our trust in God, because there have been a lot of tears.

Sometimes I find myself wishing for more, because I want to give you the sun, the moon, and the stars. I want to be enough for you. I don't know when that house will come, but I won't allow my longing for more to get in the way of finding happiness now.

The truth is, I don't know how long we'll live here. We've made memories here, and we'll continue making them.

It's true our life doesn't look how I planned, but it is beautiful. And most of all, my home will always be with you.

Estephanie Phelps is a wife and a mom to a wild toddler. She has taught abroad and now gets to explore with her little one.

You Are
My Keepsake

MEHR LEE

✕

Our house is quiet, as it tends to be these days.

The kids are out with friends, so I take it upon myself to make for a wild Friday night . . . organizing the cellar, of course.

The grumpy, old wooden staircase groans underfoot as I make my way into the darkness. At the bottom, I reach through the spiderweb-strewn rafters to find the pull chain. With a jangling click, a single bulb illuminates the basement.

Holiday decorations sit in one corner, old end tables with camping equipment in another. Stacks upon stacks of hard plastic containers litter the entire space. I shake my head. *What a mess.* This disapproval is mostly aimed at myself for letting it get so out of hand down here. I decide tackling the containers will be my first project.

I pick out the first one in arm's reach. As I examine the dust-caked lid, a red warning flag raises in my mind, but I brush it aside. I know I shouldn't open it, but the contents are calling to me. This is my boy's keepsake box.

Without thinking, I make my way to the stone floor, sitting crisscross-applesauce and holding the box tenderly in my lap as if it were my child. It kind of is.

This box holds in it the essence of my little boy.

As I peel back the lid and peak inside, I'm pummeled by a wave of nostalgia. I allow the surge to wash me out into a sea of memories.

My hand drifts over the cover of my son's baby book. Before I can stop myself, I'm fingering through the pages. Here I find an inkblot stain of his footprint. I place my hand beside it. Had his feet really been that small? Today his sneakers are the length of my forearm.

The next page holds a picture of him taking his first bath. My son—his entire body cradled in my forearm. I gaze at the picture. A head of downy black hair rests in my palm, while little legs and tiny feet dangle over each side of my arm.

Could I ever have imagined then that in the blink of an eye, I'd be the tiny one in *his* embrace? I lay the book down and continue to swim through the memories.

A lone black cowboy boot catches my eye. Looking at it now, I imagine one might see it as a worthless heap of wrinkled, faded leather. To me, it's a priceless treasure. You see, my boy wore those boots for years. Everywhere—to the grocery store, to parties, to holidays. I can still hear them clicking across our kitchen floor. I can picture him in just a diaper, those cowboy boots, a Superman cape, and a pair of toy safety goggles.

I hold the boot to my chest in an attempt to imprint this memory on my heart. I always said I was going to dip the boot in silver, but looking at the curls of black leather pulling away from the surface, I think I like it as is.

As I set the boot back in the box, another piece of leather brushes against my hand. This might be the one that drowns me. I pull out my little guy's tiny baseball glove with his first homerun ball tucked inside. *This.* This is what I think of most when I look back on his childhood: a boy and his ball. From the moment he woke in the morning until he made his way to bed at night, he always had that ball in hand. Still does.

I dig deeper into the box. With each hat, each jersey, each drawing, each trophy, each picture, I find myself desperately trying to grasp remnants of my baby boy.

The tears are flowing now, because I can't help but think, *I'll never get this back.*

I'll never cradle that little boy in my arms again, never dance along with the click of his cowboy boots, never sweep him up as he comes running from the dugout.

He won't ever need me like this again.

Just then, I hear the muffled sound of a door closing. It breaks the spell of my reverie.

I hear heavy footsteps overhead, rattling dust from the rafters.

"Mom?" the voice of a man calls from the stairway.

I almost don't recognize it because I've just been lost in memories of a little boy with a tiny voice.

I quickly replace the lid and put the container back into its place, tucking memories back where they now belong.

The past. Keepsakes.

I make my way to the bottom of the steps and look up to see my son. My boy.

The one whose footprint was smaller than my thumb.

The one who fit in the crook of my arm.

The one who strutted across my kitchen in a diaper and cowboy boots.

The one who ran to me after cracking his first home run.

The one who fit into each of those shirts, each of those frames, each of those memories.

The one who's outgrown all that's held within that box.

The one who now stands at the top of the stairwell, a head taller than his mama.

As I walk up the stairs, I think I'm walking away from my little boy. But as I reach the top step, he takes me up in a hug, and suddenly I realize the truth of it all: my little boy is not tucked away in that box with a dusty lid.

He's still there. He's right here. All wrapped up in larger-than-the-past packaging.

He's outgrown everything in that box, but he'll never outgrow my love. And that's the real keepsake.

This boy—all he was, all he is, and all he will be—fits snug in his mama's heart . . . for always.

Mehr Lee is the writer behind the blog *Raise Her Wild*. Her heart is happiest in the mountains, alongside her beautiful children and loving husband.

PART 6

SO GOD MADE A MOTHER

faithful

✕

"PLEASE GOD, LET MY CHILDREN KNOW,
NO MATTER HOW CROWDED IT GETS,
NO MATTER HOW LOUD OR CONFUSING
OR EXHAUSTING IT BECOMES, THERE IS
ALWAYS SPACE FOR THEM IN THIS PEW."

LESLIE MEANS

The Pew

LESLIE MEANS

There's a pew in our church where we sit. It's not reserved, and it doesn't hold any special markings or signs to designate our space, but nearly every Sunday, you'll find us there.

It's on the right-hand side, one row from the front. This is our pew.

If we see you in our seat, you must be new, because we know everyone around us too. It will make us pause for a moment, but don't worry—we're glad you're there anyway.

For many years my husband and I have sat in this pew. At first it was just us—a young married couple, eager to begin our life together in a new community. We sat in that pew, hand in hand, listening to the sermon, finding peace on Sunday mornings.

It's where I prayed for our marriage, for my husband. For jobs and decisions. It's where I prayed God would bless us with children.

And the babies came.

Our first daughter, and then another just twenty-three months later. The girls made our pew a bit tighter . . . and much louder. Sunday mornings stopped being a time of rest and relaxation, and more of an exhausting chore.

The baby would cry, the toddler would yell. My husband and I would take turns leaving the pew with one squirming child in our arms, sometimes both.

But still, nearly every Sunday, we sat in that pew.

Eventually the girls grew older and began listening. Our pew became calm again and my prayers more earnest. *Please watch over these girls. Please protect them as they grow. Please don't let me screw this up.*

We watched Christmas programs and Sunday-morning bell choirs, Easter sunrise services and summer Bible school skits from that pew. Some mornings I could feel God's presence so closely it was like He was sitting next to me. Other mornings I would be so frustrated with God I couldn't even get my mind to tell Him hello.

Today our pew holds five. My husband, me, our two daughters, and one very rambunctious little boy.

You'll find cracker crumbs on the cushions and stains in the corner. There are pencil marks and scribbled papers and a few ripped pages in the hymnals. We're back to where we were a few years ago—taking turns removing a very loud child from his seat—and sitting between two sisters who like to bicker. Most mornings it's exhausting just being there.

And yet we still go.

Because I know how important it is to sit in that pew. Years ago, my parents did the same thing. We sat on the right-hand side, one row from the front. I didn't always understand the sermon or even why we had to go every Sunday.

But I get it now.

I got lost for a while. Somewhere between age sixteen until age twenty-four, God and I had a distant relationship. If I sat in a pew, I certainly wasn't talking to Him.

But He was always talking to me. Waiting for me to find my way back to my seat in His church.

Would I be sitting in the pew today if Mom and Dad hadn't been so consistent with us all those years ago?

I can't be sure. Today, my prayers in that pew are well worn. *Please God, don't let me mess this up. Please let me love them enough. Please help me be a good wife, a good mother, a good friend, a good daughter.*

And I've added this one: *Please God, let my children know, no matter how crowded it gets, no matter how loud or confusing or exhausting it becomes, there is always space for them in this pew.*

Because isn't that what we long for as mothers? For our kids to sit beside us in that pew as long as we have them, soaking up Jesus and our admittedly imperfect faith—until one day they find themselves praying those same prayers for their own kids?

No matter where you are today, I pray these next few stories meet you there and fill you with hope.

Can You Stay
with Me Tonight?

MEG DUNCAN

×

She asked me to stay with her that night, but I couldn't.

Not only did I have to work in the morning, but the next day was Valentine's Day, and we had to make sure each student had an envelope with a special Buzz Lightyear pencil taped to it. Plus, only moments before, my second grader reminded me I'd signed up to bring twenty-four cupcakes and read a story to his class for the party.

I wanted to kick the me of last August, who'd gone to the teacher meet-and-greet and signed my name to some obligation that felt really far away at the time.

So I kissed my mom's forehead and told her that tomorrow was a big day—and it was.

Mom had advanced lung cancer, and the only facility that had space to care for her was about forty-five minutes from me. I was there every evening after work, but with my husband's schedule, I couldn't stay with her many nights.

Finally, a medical facility only a few minutes away from my house had an opening. My husband was taking the next day off so we could move her there, and my plan was to be by her side around the clock.

The truth was, I was emotionally exhausted. We were all still mourning my dad, who had died two months earlier from pancreatic cancer, and while I was hanging on by a thread myself, I knew Mom's struggle was worse than mine. So

I packed up my pain, knowing I'd be unpacking it again soon, since hospice had given Mom about eight weeks to live.

She smiled and nodded and grabbed my hand, holding it as tightly as she could. I looked down and studied her hand for a moment. The same hand that once guided me through life, and even whacked my bottom every now and then, was now so frail. I gave it a gentle squeeze.

As I got up to leave, she called my name, and I stopped at the door. "Megs," she said (her favorite nickname for me), "I love you with all my heart. You have made me so happy."

I smiled and told her I couldn't wait to see her the next night.

The call came at 4:30 a.m., and I sat straight up in bed at its ring. My stomach started churning when I saw the number and noticed the time. The nurse's voice, though compassionate, sliced right through my heart.

"Your mom passed away," she said. "We believe it was a few hours ago."

"She was supposed to have two months left," I said, my voice firm. "Hospice said so."

I wasn't sure if I was telling the nurse or telling God. I just wanted someone in charge to know the timing was all wrong. It wasn't supposed to happen this way. I was going to breathe that last breath with her, just like I did with my dad.

And I would have, if I'd have stayed like she'd asked.

I replay that scene in my mind at the oddest times. When I'm driving home from work. In the grocery checkout line. One time right when I started screaming on the downhill slope of a roller coaster ride.

Can you stay with me tonight?

Regret washes over me, and all the same questions flood my mind.

Did she know she was going to die that night?

Did she think I didn't care?

Was she afraid?

I can't bear the thought of her being alone and scared. But then God reminds me she wasn't alone.

He planned her departure just as carefully as He planned her arrival. He knew

I wouldn't be there, and for some reason He didn't want me to be. I think He might have wanted some time alone with her before she left this world.

Mom was pretty mad at God for taking my dad and for the months of sickness they both endured before he died. Even before that, Mom had suffered with agoraphobia and life-altering OCD, not leaving the house for years at a time, and she often blamed God when she isolated herself.

Mom and God had some things to work out, and I believe I needed to go home and tend to my children so He could tend to His. Perhaps He even put a little bug in my ear at the teacher meet-and-greet to sign up for those cupcakes— although I've done that three more times since (darn you again, Meg of August).

When regret creeps in, I remember God has plans that sometimes don't make sense to anyone but Him. So when those same old questions start to replay in my mind, I instead remind myself of her last words to me.

"Megs," she said—oh how I miss hearing her voice say that sweet nickname!— "I love you with all my heart. You have made me so happy."

Those words were sent from Jesus to Mom's lips—and straight to my heart.

Meg Duncan is the author of *Life on Saturn: A Lifetime of Grace in Unexpected Places* and writes the award-winning newspaper column What a Life.

When God Whispers

DEBBIE PRATHER

It had never happened before, and it hasn't happened since: God smacked me over the head with a fat, heavy, rolled-up newspaper. At least, that's exactly how it felt.

And believe me, He had my full attention, because immediately afterward, I heard with complete clarity the word *adoption*.

My jaw dropped and apparently I looked stunned, because the women sitting around me asked, "What?"

I didn't have words.

We were at a women's retreat and had just listened to a dynamic speaker talk about how God often whispers in our ears, prompting us to some kind of action, but we tend to brush Him off, not entirely convinced or convicted. The speaker ended her talk with a poignant question, directed at the women packed in the large ballroom, a question that hung in the air for a moment before I felt the life-changing, undeniable thump. The question was, "What is God leading you to do?"

My husband and I had thought about adoption a handful of times through-out our then-twelve-year marriage. He'd been adopted into his loving family as a newborn, and even though at times we thought God was calling us to expand our family in the same way, our lives were already crazy with two active little boys.

But that day, God commanded my focus—and He continued to do so, because when I arrived home and told my husband the story, my wise, never-impulsive better half didn't flinch for one second.

Instead, he said, "Let's do it!"

Now it was my turn to say, "Wait . . . what?"

"We're not getting any younger," he added. "If this is how God wants us to have another child, we'd better get going."

My heart pounded in fear but also excitement, and somehow I knew God's plan was already in motion.

We had no idea where to start, but we soon met a couple at our kids' swim meet who had adopted their son and daughter from Russia. They said they couldn't have been happier with their adoption agency and gave us the information.

We took it as a sign and made contact the next day. We learned that to adopt from that country, we'd have to make two separate week-long trips, flying more than twelve hours each way, and we wouldn't be allowed to bring our sons. With my fear of flying and knowing we'd have to leave our children home, I quickly ruled out the idea.

God needed to grab my attention again.

The day after talking to the agency and deciding we'd look elsewhere, a repairman arrived at our home to install a new light fixture. His name was Vladimir, and he told me he was from Moscow.

The following day, I was trying on clothes and an employee asked if she could take some extras out of the dressing room. After hearing her accent, I asked where she was from. I knew the answer before she said it.

The third day, I met a young mom at an auto repair shop who was reading a book to her daughter. The little girl smiled and played peekaboo from behind the pages.

"What a sweetheart she is," I told her mom.

"We still can't believe how lucky we are," she said. "We adopted her from Russia last year."

God was no longer whispering in my ear—He was yelling.

I called the same agency the next day and began the paperwork. There were many highs and lows throughout the tedious, emotional process of adopting our daughter, and there have been joys and challenges while raising all three of our children. Our sons are now grown and married and thinking about children of their own, and our baby girl is a senior in high school, dreaming of her future.

I still don't have words to express how grateful we are for the God-whisper in that big, crowded room almost twenty years ago. I've prayed each day since my heart will listen for His voice and I will continually ponder, *What is God leading me to do?*

Debbie Prather shares her words of wisdom at *742 i love you* and recently completed her yet-unpublished novel, *For You and For Me.*

His Widow, Their Mother

NICOLE HASTINGS

✕

It's 2 a.m. and I'm awake. I know my two-day-old baby girl will be awake soon to fill her growling little tummy. I just crawled back into my bed in the living room ten minutes ago, and my eyes can't shut because someone will need me again soon. When I finish feeding the baby, one or both of my two-year-old twin boys will awaken with night terrors they haven't been able to shake since their whole world turned upside down.

When I finally get the toddlers back to bed, I'll see our bedroom light turn on from across the hall and I'll need to help my dying husband. My thirty-four-year-old dying husband, whose cancer is slowly stealing him from us. I'll hold the trash can as he gets sick in it. I'll empty his bedpan into the toilet. I'll struggle to remember how much morphine to give him. I'll wipe his clammy forehead with a warm washcloth and hold his hand.

For a minute, I'll just be his wife and not his nurse. He'll hold me in his arms until he becomes too weak and I have to hold him in mine. For just a minute, life will seem normal and I'll just be an exhausted mom, like all the other exhausted moms on the planet, going through the same routine: feeding babies and putting them back to bed at 2 a.m.

But my eyes will steal away to the glaring red numbers on the alarm clock on my husband's nightstand, and I'll know I have only a few minutes before I have to leave him in our marriage bed—now his deathbed—and head back to my makeshift bed in the living room to check on the baby and maybe, just maybe, get a moment of rest before the cycle begins again.

There will come a day when I'll trade my living room bed for a borrowed hospital bed in the hospice facility, where my husband will spend his last few days. The twins will be taken care of by Grandma and Papa, another bittersweet relief, as our family will be taken care of but separated. I'll be relieved to have my own hospital room to share with my two-week-old baby, complete with a door that shuts—a luxury I haven't had in months.

The cycle will consist of waking to feed and change the baby, then plodding across the cold linoleum to sit with the man whose hand I vowed to hold in sickness and in health. I will hold his hand while holding our daughter in the crook of my arm while silence fills the room, broken only by intermittent, rattling breaths from my husband and beeps, clicks, and drips from IV bags and medical machines.

Then there will come a time when I walk barefoot across the linoleum to his room one last time. Only that time, I will thrust my baby into the nurse's arms to sit beside the man I love as he takes his final breath.

The room will fill with silence. The machines will be turned off. A wail will be heard. As startling as it is, I'll realize the sound is coming from me. I'll be his wife for just a moment longer while I can still feel the warmth of his hand and I can still hear his heartbeat as I lay my sobbing head on his chest.

My eyes will look to the closed hospital door, and I'll know my baby girl is waiting for me on the other side. I'll look at the body of the man who was once my husband and burn into my memory his stillness, the peace on his face now that he is no longer suffering. I will stop crying and take a deep breath that hurts all my insides as my heart shatters into a million pieces. I will rise from the chair and start toward the door, never looking back at the hospital bed again. I will open the hospital door and see the nurse holding my girl. I will take my baby, and we will walk back to our room together. I will feed her and feel her warmth.

A few hours later, I will walk out of the hospital no longer a wife but a widow.

I will go home to my little boys and reunite them with their baby sister. I will feed them dinner, bathe them, read them bedtime stories, and tuck them in.

I will rock my baby to sleep. Then I'll put her down in her crib and stand by to watch her dream. I'll walk slowly back to the bed I have reclaimed as my own, trying to avoid the vast emptiness of "his" side, and shut my eyes for just a moment, until the cycle begins again. And I'll remember I am exactly who God chose me to be: the mother to these children.

Nicole Hastings is happily married to her "second chapter" and a proud mom of three, plus two bonus kiddos—proof that God works all things together for good.

Mothering a Child with Anxiety

ELIZABETH SPENCER

Mothering a child with anxiety caught me completely off guard.

Like everyone else on the planet who's breathing, I have my own list of struggles and challenges, but anxiety has never been one of them. My siblings didn't battle it, nor did my husband. Neither of my children exhibited any readily identifiable signs of worrisome anxiousness during their younger years.

So when my seventeen-year-old daughter asked for help finding a counselor to deal with anxiety, I felt like nominating myself for a lifetime achievement award in the "worst mom ever" category.

How had I missed this? How hadn't I seen the signs? As my daughter uncovered and dealt with her anxiety and shared pieces of her past, things suddenly made sense in the light of this new understanding (the river float trip for her birthday when she sobbed her way down the river comes to mind).

I told her, "I'm so sorry I didn't know about this. I'm sorry I didn't recognize it."

But my daughter reassured me, "Mom, it's not your fault. I didn't know about it either."

When you know better, you do better, so since my daughter's diagnosis, I've tried to do just that. I'm trying to be a good (or at least passing) student in the school of parenting a child with anxiety, and I'm trying to apply these lessons well (even if my daughter admittedly often has to grade me on a curve).

I've learned to accept some new realities:

- Our kids can be well loved and still be anxious.
- They can come from secure homes and still be anxious.
- They can be reasonably scheduled and still be anxious.
- They can have good friends and still be anxious.
- They can have strong faith and still be anxious.
- They can be covered in prayer and still be anxious.
- They can be getting enough sleep and still be anxious.
- They can have a happy childhood and still be anxious.
- They can be excited for their future and still be anxious.
- They can have realistic expectations for themselves and still be anxious.
- They can be good but not overly pressured students and still be anxious.

I learned anxiety is no respecter of schedules or finances or grades or family dynamics or social status.

I learned I could play a part in removing the stigma of anxiety. I needed to respect my daughter's privacy, but when she granted me permission to share about her journey, I owed it to her to do so in a way that didn't paint anxiety as something to be ashamed of or embarrassed about—because what would that tell my anxious daughter about how I felt about her?

I learned to remind my daughter she wasn't the only one fighting anxiety—not by a long shot. I assured her that if she chose to share this part of herself with others, it wouldn't scare them off. In fact, it would probably make them feel less frightened of their own battles.

I learned that while it was important to address the causes of my daughter's anxiety, I needed to spend less time trying to figure out who and what were to blame and more time supporting my daughter, guiding her, finding helpful resources, adjusting details of her life as necessary, and loving her more fiercely than ever.

I learned to ask some new questions.

"Is it going to increase your anxiety if I [fill in the blank]?"

"What don't I know about having anxiety that you think I need to know?"

"What have I done lately that has made your anxiety worse?"

"What have I done lately that has eased your anxiety?"

I learned to help my daughter focus less on asking what was wrong with her and more on claiming all that's right with her. Her strengths. Her talents. Her victories. Her perseverance. Her compassion. Her bravery. Her determination. Her dreams. Her goals. Her hope.

And above all, her willingness to do what it takes—with my often-clumsy help, support, and reinforcement of truth—to get to the place where she can say and believe, "I have anxiety, but it does not have me. Anxiety is part of my life right now, but it is not the whole of it. I am anxious sometimes, but that is not all of who I am all the time. And who I am, both with and without anxiety, is someone the world needs me to be."

Elizabeth Spencer is a wife and "roomier nest" mom. She writes as *Guilty Chocoholic Mama* and is author of the devotional *Known By His Names*.

The Power
of a Legacy

KIM HOWARD

My mother-in-law died about nine years after I met her, but I never really knew her—not the real her, at least. By the time my husband and I met, she was battling Alzheimer's disease.

In the beginning, she would carry on short conversations with me. We exchanged small talk about nothing, really, and our interactions were always polite, with lots of smiles. She was quiet, tagging along in conversations and outings—nothing like the way she was often described to me.

People told me she was a force. Strong. Confident. Faithful. Funny. A prayer warrior. Capable. Trusted. A teacher. A leader. A business owner. She had a sly sense of humor and a truckload of sass. I always wished I could have known the real her.

As the years went on, she slowly lost her ability to communicate. I mourned all the missed conversations and memories we should have been making.

I felt the loss of her most profoundly when my husband and I had kids. She would have been the one always at our house to help. She would have fought for a turn to hold the babies, then hogged them the whole time. The help would have been wonderful, but having someone who loved our babies so fiercely, jealous for more time with them—there's no way to put that incredible feeling into words.

My heart will always ache that she couldn't be that person for my kids and that they didn't get to experience the full force of her love.

I feel the hole in my life from her absence in many ways, and it seems like new ways are always popping up, surprising me and breaking my heart all over again. Like the time I was talking with her sister about my worries over how small our third baby was. He was in the third percentile for weight, and I was forever anxious about it. She said, "Don't worry! Brian was small too! He'll grow. He'll be fine. You know, when Brian was little and he would say he was hungry, no matter what time of the day it was, Pam would stop what she was doing and make him a sandwich."

That story, however small, is one I should have gotten from my mother-in-law. I should be hearing anecdotes firsthand and taking comfort in her gentle reassurance. I'm so grateful my husband's aunt shared it with me, and I'm greedy for more stories like that.

While it's easy to think about all the things I don't have without her in my life, there is one precious thing I do have—and, oh, I am so thankful for it. When my husband talks about his memories of his mother, the strongest ones are of her on her knees in her bedroom, praying. What a picture to remember someone by. What a testament to her faith-filled life.

Once I was talking to my husband about how crazy it was that I became a Christian in high school. Nothing about my life to that point would have guided me toward the Lord. He said, "My mom used to pray for you."

I knew then. The one thing I've always had from the real her—the one thing I still have from her—is her legacy of prayer.

Kim Howard is the picture book author of *Do Mommies Ever Sleep?* and *Grace and Box*. She is a mom to three kids.

Why Us?

MISSY HILLMER

×

I'd just gotten ready for bed that Friday night when my husband, Bill, got an uneasy feeling. Our teenage son, Tyler, was late—he was supposed to be home from hanging out with his friends by now. My husband just knew something was wrong. We both tried calling Tyler, with no answer. Bill left to look for the boys; I sat there expecting my son to call and say he and his friends had simply lost track of time.

It wasn't until the call came from my frantic husband that I knew something was terribly wrong.

There had been an accident about a mile from our house—and it was bad.

I hung up the phone and fell to the floor. For a split second, I was paralyzed. Then God equipped me with strength, focus, and a calm enough voice to call 911. My parents were visiting that weekend, which meant there was someone to stay home with our sleeping daughter while I left the house. This felt like a small mercy from God.

I remember asking God to be with us as my dad drove my older son and me to the scene of the accident, uncertain of what we'd find once we got there.

When we arrived, my husband was holding Tyler. He was gone. My older son prayed for God to help him, to fix him, to make this nightmare go away. I remember watching Tyler lying there peacefully when I felt someone lift me from where I sat and move me to the middle of the country road, even though there was no one close by.

I stood alone, looking at the full moon, then closed my eyes. I felt a gentle breeze and heard these words: *Everything is going to be okay.* Tyler often said these exact words to calm me when I was worked up over something. I've never felt more peace than I did at that moment. I have no doubt it was a divine appointment arranged by God.

It wasn't until Bill and I were walking home hours later that I remember him saying, "Why? Why us? This doesn't happen to people like us—now what do we do?"

These were good questions—raw, real, and incomprehensible. How were we even talking about this? Just a half hour—that was all the time he was supposed to be gone. Now we were going through the unimaginable.

The accident happened three days after Tyler turned fifteen. He was a kind, caring, hardworking young man who would do anything for anyone. It didn't make sense.

But God spoke to me loud and clear again: *Why not you?* And it's true—why not us? Who are we to think we would be immune to pain?

Back home in the shower, water fell gently on my head. I closed my eyes and tried to forget what had happened, reminding myself to breathe. I felt numb as tears flowed down my face. Was this really happening, or was it just a dream? But the nightmare was real. My precious blue-eyed boy was not coming home.

A dear friend who lost her husband once told me it was okay to cry—that tears have a way of healing us, and the best place to do this is in the shower. The first few days after Tyler's accident, that's what I did. I cried in the shower, where there were no interruptions, no questions, no people—just cleansing water and quietness. I talked to God, repeatedly asking Him, *Why? What did I do wrong to make You take my son?*

Almost a decade later, I still don't have a satisfying answer to the "Why?" question. But I do have an answer to the "Who?" question. God was with Tyler that night. He was with me that night. And He is still with me now.

Missy Hillmer navigates the loss of her son Tyler through her faith in God. She encourages and supports others at *The Blue Eyed Dragonfly.*

I Pray for My Children

JACLYN WARREN

×

I hear my children giggling as they play, and I know they won't be this little for long. I have two garbage bags filled with clothes they've outgrown just this summer. A mama knows what happens when she blinks.

Time has given us so much. A full camera roll and shoeboxes stuffed with souvenirs and love notes prove it. But time has also taken so much. I can't remember the last time I carried my oldest son to bed. I miss those days we stayed cuddled on the couch as I rocked him to sleep. I could feel the weight of love reaching out to squeeze my hand and hug me back.

So many of my favorite days have become memories.

Their sweet baby faces are changing, yet I can still see each younger version of them when I look closely enough. As we count down another year, they're walking a bit farther away and becoming a little less dependent on me.

So I pray.

I ask God to help me be the mom they need in the season they're facing. I ask God to draw me close so I can guide my children closer to Him.

I pray for my children to be armed with the full protection of God.

I pray for my children to stand firm in their faith.

I thank God for His goodness in each hug and high five.

I thank God for making me their mom.

These are the prayers I whispered over my growing belly before we had any names picked out. The same prayers I'll murmur until the end of my days.

I would do anything for the well-being of my children, but God *can* do anything. So I'll keep going to my knees in battle for my family.

I pray before bedtime when they can hear me, and I pray when I come back to check on them after they've fallen asleep.

I pray when I'm rubbing my sleepy eyes over my morning coffee.

I pray when terror on the news takes my breath away.

I know I'm not the one who holds the future; I'm a mom who wants to give my children the very best. So every day, I pray.

Before my third son was a month old, he was diagnosed with RSV and I had to call 911 multiple times. I couldn't understand why this beautiful, perfect child had to struggle so hard to breathe. I remember his pediatrician telling me to watch his skin to see if his color changed. I felt helpless. The only thing I could do was trust Jesus. I sang "Jesus Loves Me" as the monitors beeped. And I prayed.

I thanked God for His healing and for the way He provides. Yet I struggled to overcome the panicked feeling that something else was wrong. I traded reality for worst-case scenarios. I couldn't focus. I couldn't make lunch. I couldn't drive without getting distracted. I needed help.

I called my doctor. And I prayed.

There were first days of school. There were new friends. There were tantrums—so many tantrums. There were broken bones and so many unknowns. But God has been faithful to calm me when I reach for His hand in prayer.

I want my children to be strong and courageous. So I pray.

I want my children to have a relationship with the living God. So I pray.

I want my children to know they are loved and valued. So I pray.

My babies are turning into young men quicker than I ever thought possible. My oldest just skipped from size 8 in kids' clothes to size 10, and I wonder where the ninth year has gone.

I question if I'm a good enough mom, if I'm doing it right, if I'm present enough, if I'm going to mess up somehow.

I want my children to choose good friends.

I want them to know Jesus.

I want them to trust God.

So I pray.

The enemy's arrows are coming straight for all of us. But I want my children to always remember that in God, they will find refuge—that no matter what tomorrow brings, God is good. So we can trust Him . . . and pray.

Jaclyn Warren created the blog *mommy's 15 minutes* to scrapbook life with her children and encourage mamas to pause and savor God's goodness in motherhood.

PART 7

SO GOD MADE A MOTHER

worthy

DOUBT SAYS,

Am I a good mom? Did they feel my love today? Am I doing it all wrong?

TRUTH ANSWERS,

I am exactly the mother my children need, and no one else could love them better.

HER VIEW FROM HOME

The Love

LESLIE MEANS

✕

I bought Cocoa Puffs today. You know, that chocolate breakfast cereal that shouldn't count as breakfast because it's really just a dessert, but oh my gosh, it's good. Not good *for* you, but good. Every time I buy this cereal, I remember my past.

I didn't have much as a kid. Name-brand shoes? Forget about it. Fancy vacations? Does a tent made of bedsheets hanging from the clothesline count? Cable? Hardly. Air conditioning? Why would we pay for that when we had perfectly good windows?

You get my point. We weren't poor, but we weren't rich, either. We were your typical middle class (maybe lower middle class, depending on the year) family.

I was the kid who showed sheep at the county fair wearing fabric shoes from the half-price store (remember that place?). The other kids wore fancy boots with rhinestones, of course.

I was the kid who wore hand-me-downs from my sisters and got my hair cut by Mom at home and helped clip coupons to save a few cents each Saturday.

We froze food so it didn't spoil, and you'd better believe we finished what was on our plates.

We didn't participate in the traveling sports teams or drama clubs or acting camps because we didn't have a money tree readily available.

My first car was a 1983 two-tone green LTD—driven first by my grandma and then by my sister. By the time the car finally reached me, it was so worn out the muffler fell off during a rousing cruise downtown. It also died at every stop sign and fogged up the windows with some kind of white smoke I likely shouldn't have inhaled.

And my favorite name-brand cereal, Cocoa Puffs? We rarely ate it. Because generic cereal was cheaper. And it came with coupons.

Nope, we didn't have much on paper. I was just a girl who grew up in the eighties and nineties on a farm in the middle of Nebraska.

At least, that's what you might see. But the reality was different.

Here's what I remember: church on Sunday mornings. Meat, potatoes, canned pickles, and bread, served at our table every Sunday after the service. A mother who worked long hours but still managed to attend every school event. A father who would (and likely did) give the shirt off his back to a stranger in need. Hardworking parents who gave back to our community, welcomed friends into our home, worked the land, and cared for animals. Prayers every night, without fail. A house full of love.

The world tries to tell us we need to do more, be more. We feel pressure to fill our days with *busy* so we can look important, crush our goals, and make big money. And we have to share it all on social media to prove to our friends and family we've made something of ourselves.

We want the fancy Cocoa Puffs.

I get it—I'm a dreamer. I like to set goals and work hard too. And it's clear I want those Cocoa Puffs every now and then.

But I can't help but think about my childhood—that simple girl from a humble home. I really was so happy. And I'm still so happy.

Know why? Because Mom and Dad loved me. We didn't have a lot, but we had enough. And we were cherished. I've felt that love every day for forty years. It's been with me when I had a little and when I had a lot, and it keeps me thankful for every dang thing I have.

Including that box of Cocoa Puffs.

That might sound simple, but maybe that's exactly what we're missing today: simple.

Friend, the true beauty of motherhood comes when we get real about what matters. When we focus on loving our people well and doing the best we can, with what we have, where we are. When we let go of the ridiculous idea of perfection and realize God has made us worthy of this calling.

As you read these stories, I hope you'll know, deep in your bones, that motherhood has never been about being perfect or about what someone else says it should be. It's always been about love.

I Don't Do It All, and You Don't Have to Either

DEB PRESTON

✕

I spent the first thirty years of my life trying to please everyone. I said yes to everything, even if I didn't have the time or the mental bandwidth, even if I didn't want to.

I resented a lot of the things I felt compelled to do. I resented the people who pushed past my boundaries. *But at least they like me,* I'd tell myself.

My daughter's birth added more pressure. Now I was severely sleep deprived, overwhelmed by uncertainty, and tormented by the need to avoid failure at all costs.

And so I kept doing. I attended parent-child classes and story times and playdates and all the things you're "supposed" to do for your child's development.

I made long road trips to visit family and friends, even when I was exhausted, even when my daughter was moody and difficult. Because what kind of person would I be if I didn't attend my niece's birthday party six hours away?

When I returned to work after four years at home, I thought for certain I would break. I was waking up early to care for my daughter and assist my husband through a difficult diagnosis. I cooked and cleaned and ran all our household errands. And then at 3 p.m., I'd start my full-time job. I'd drive to the office and work until midnight, only to do it all over again the next day.

In the midst of it all, I pressured myself to continue doing *everything*. We attended swim classes and T-ball practices. I volunteered at my daughter's school. (If I wasn't technically doing anything at the time they needed help, I was obligated to help . . . right? If I didn't, what would they think of me?) I led a biweekly Bible study, launched a writing career, and just *had* to host family and friends at least twice a month.

During this time, I often imagined myself dying on the spot, grabbing my chest and falling to the ground, overwhelmed and finally done in by my workload. My family and friends would shake their heads knowingly, not at all surprised by my fate.

"She was the strongest person I knew," they'd whisper sadly to one another.

It was a phrase I'd heard often. I used to take it as a compliment, as it was intended. But I began considering it an omen—one that shouldn't be ignored.

And so I stopped. I began to draw lines in the sand, boundaries to protect myself from the certain fate of collapsing one day.

I limited my daughter's extracurricular activities to just one or two per year: one sports season, one club—that was more than enough stimulation for a young mind. I decided to value her time at home as an opportunity to rest, relax, connect with family, and cultivate creativity.

I stopped leading a Bible study out of obligation. I realized my true passion for ministry was writing, so I did that more.

I turned down volunteering at my daughter's school. I recognized just how precious those three hours a day were to my mental health—and that my mental health should be a priority.

I declined countless events and activities when they weren't feasible for me or my family. I said no to events where, even if our schedule allowed, the heat or crowd would make the experience unenjoyable. One ninety-five-degree-day pumpkin patch meltdown is enough for us, thank you very much.

I reminded myself that roads travel in both directions. We made trips to visit family when it was possible and let them visit us as well.

I stopped carrying my phone around the house. I no longer raced to answer calls I didn't have time to take, knowing I could call people back when I was able to give them my full attention and answer texts when I had time.

Some people didn't like it at first. And whether it was true or not, I felt they didn't like *me* because of it. But then I realized I can only do what's right and best and, frankly, possible for my family and me. I can control my own actions, but I can't control other people's reactions to them.

If others are upset I've set boundaries to protect my physical and mental health, that's on them. It's something I can't change, and I've learned to be okay with that. Because ultimately, they're not working until midnight to pay my bills or driving my daughter to T-ball practice or paying for my medical care when I neglect my health. They won't be the ones to collapse on the floor on the path to doing it all.

I used to do it all—and it made me miserable. Now I do a few things very well, and I enjoy maintaining control of my own time, energy, and mental health.

Ultimately, God is the only One we're called to please. And honoring Him makes all the difference.

Deb Preston is a wife, mother, editor, and award-winning author of *Girls Can*. She regularly writes about parenting, faith, and health on her blog.

The Unseen Work You're Doing Matters

KELSEY SCISM

✕

Hey, stay-at-home mom. Yeah, I'm talking to you, the one with the stained shirt, Cheerios in your hair, and the color-coded calendar that looks like a rainbow threw up. It's a lot, isn't it? This stay-at-home mom thing—to be a diaper changer, laundry folder, meal prepper, taxi driver, and tear catcher all day, every day.

It's funny how it can feel like too much and yet not enough at the same time. I know you love being the one who gets to support, encourage, and care for your kids. But still, you sort of wonder if there's something more. Sometimes your heart silently cries, *God, is this all You have planned for me?*

Yes, you know the most important thing a mama can do is raise her babies. You know the work you're doing inside your walls is really Kingdom work. You know you're building the world changers of the next generation. You know all that.

But some days it still feels so insignificant and mundane.

What if this isn't it?

What if there's more?

What if God has a purpose for you alongside raising your babies?

In the midst of the everyday tasks of motherhood, God wants to use you in ways that reach beyond your own four walls.

Sweet stay-at-home mother, you were created to be a mom. You were created for these kids. And right beside motherhood you have a unique purpose: to love, serve, and encourage all God's people, not just the ones He's placed in your arms.

As you walk behind the stroller, pushing the toddler who will only sit still when strapped in, you can pray. Pray for the neighbors whose houses you stroll by. Pray for your community. Pray for the mama across the street or the mama across the world. Your heavenly Father walks beside that stroller, listening to each word you pray.

As you make yet another meal to feed your hungry horde, maybe you can make a second one. The mess is already there—it doesn't take much more work to throw in two of everything. That meal can give relief to another family barely making it through the week. You get it; you've been there. The extra pan could bring nourishment to the quiet, elderly couple down the street—not just for their stomachs, but for their souls. God stands beside you at the stovetop as you serve and love the people He's placed in your life.

As your child colors at the kitchen table, pick up a marker yourself. Grab a piece of stationery, a cute card, or one of your little artist's creations, and write an encouraging note. Maybe it's to a teacher, a bus driver, or the clerk at the grocery store you seem to visit every day. You'll know who . . . God will sit beside you and whisper that person's name to your heart.

As you wait in line—the school pickup, the store, the gas station, the library—search for a compliment to give. "Hey, I like your shirt." "Thanks for being so efficient." "Your kids are sweet and kind." "You do your job so well." "You have a great smile." Honestly, the words really don't matter much. It's more about the time, the genuine effort you put into making someone else's day more beautiful. And right there, standing in line beside you, God smiles at the simple beauty of your words.

As you sit behind the wheel, teenage voices fill the air. Though you don't say much, you slip in some encouragement when the timing is right. Your simple presence influences the young people in the car—a way to show love and joy in everyday ways. Your goal may be to simply pick up or drop off safely, but God has a bigger goal as He rides beside you, revealing a little of Himself to those kids through you.

Do you see the purpose God has for you? He wants to use you where you are in this season of motherhood to bless and reach His people.

I know the days are long. I know you feel unseen in a world full of hustlers and ladder climbers and glass-ceiling breakers. But you are important. The work you do—for your children and beside them—will change lives. They're parallel purposes, equally important.

God has big things planned for you, mama, right where you are.

Kelsey Scism writes about her journey of faith and the ways God speaks to her heart on her website *Loving Our Lord.*

A Mother
Has Many Sides

BETH HOFF

✕

I launched my first business when I was ten years old. I gathered up the kids in the neighborhood and enthusiastically cast my vision. "What if"—I painted the picture for them—"we take care of people's pets while they're on vacation and they pay us money? Like, real money?"

My friends' eyes grew wide with the same excitement and anticipation they saw emanating from me. They were in.

We cut out animal-shaped clipart and printed flyers on neon pink paper advertising our pet-sitting business. Then we walked the horseshoe-shaped street I grew up on and passed out flyers to everyone we could find.

What's even more surprising is people started hiring us to watch their pets. We made three hundred dollars that summer, which to my ten-year-old self might as well have been a million.

And just like that, I was an entrepreneur.

But more than that, a huge part of who I am was born that day. Finding creative ways to solve problems and serve people makes me come alive. Some people call it work, but I say it's a calling.

When my first daughter was born, everyone asked if I would quit my job and stay home full time. After all, that's what mothers are supposed to do, right?

I felt conflicted. Family is everything to me. But deep down, I knew staying home wasn't the right choice for me. So I kept working *and* poured myself into motherhood.

After eight years as a working mom (and two daughters later), I've made an incredible discovery: working doesn't rob my kids of their best mom—it helps bring their best mom to the table.

I'm breaking glass ceilings for my daughters. I'm showing them they were made for something—that their gifts, their talents, and their hard work make a difference.

When I got promoted to chief operating officer last year, my kids cheered. We filled glasses with sparkling grape juice and celebrated together. They see the way I come alive when I'm leading a team and implementing a mission that serves thousands of elementary school teachers around the world. And they're just as proud of me as I am of them.

Every day I go to work, I'm letting my daughters see that work isn't drudgery—it's a calling. It's being part of something bigger than yourself. It's using the creativity God has given you to make a difference in the world.

Some people describe being a working mom as living in constant tension between work and family, as though these two entities are constantly battling against each other, and one (or both) is always losing.

But what if there's another possibility? What if working and being a mom aren't in competition but rather are in synergy?

The truth is, working makes me a better mom. When I go to work, I'm not just clocking hours for a paycheck. I'm accessing the person God created me to be and using what He gave me in a way that helps shape the world around me. And I love it.

When I come home from work, my kids come crashing into my arms with squeals of delight and a thousand stories to share about their day. I shower them with kisses, and we snuggle on the couch and read books and laugh together about silly things. And I love every minute of it.

I'm not choosing work over my children—I'm allowing myself to have more than one purpose in life. Not to be a mother *or*, but instead, to be a mother *and*.

Someday, if my daughters want to be stay-at-home mothers, I will celebrate and cheer them on. I will tell them that's an incredible purpose. If they want to be a teacher or a CEO or a vet or open a coffee shop or write a book, I will celebrate that, too.

And I will tell them it's possible to be an amazing mom *and* do those things. God has created you with gifts and passions and dreams, not to tease you, but because He loves you. Your family can be your number-one priority, but they don't have to be your only purpose.

Working can empower you to be a better mom, and being a mother can teach you to be a better leader at work.

You're not just a working mom. You are called. You are purposeful. You are a mother *and*.

Beth Hoff blogs about marriage, motherhood, and shaping the culture of your family at *Favorite Families* and hosts the *Family Culture* podcast.

The Greatest Gift
I Give My Children
Is Love

KATIE WEBER

The day my marriage was over was the day my love for my sons began to change.

I was heartbroken for them and for me. Every wish and dream I had for them was shattered. How was I going to give them the best life now? Divorced parents. Two homes. Parallel parenting. Back and forth. This was a life I'd never imagined.

In the face of everything, I promised my children I would give them the life they deserved and needed. So I gave them love.

It ripped my heart into pieces. Stole my breath. Radiated deep into my soul.

Selfishly, I want to hold them tight. Keep them protected in my arms. Shelter the three of us from the destruction around us. Never let them go.

But I don't.

When I'm with the boys, I pretend it doesn't hurt. I hold back the tears. I smile and reassure them. Then I let them go to be loved by others. To be held, to be kissed, to laugh and make memories, to be told "I love you"—by someone else.

I hold back every hurt, every negative thought, every ounce of bitterness, never allowing my sons to hear me speak poorly about those who love them. I work to heal the open wounds still bleeding from infidelity and divorce. And when I want to give in to the anger, when I don't want to be the bigger person, I remember my love for my children.

This love pushes me to swallow my pride, to carry the burden alone, to show up when I want to hide, to teach my sons there's a better way than living with hate.

This love won't allow me to hate someone who cares for my children. I want my kids to see, no matter the situation, no matter what happens to you or how someone treats you, you are in control of how you treat others. How you react. How you live your life. I want to show my boys what this kind of love looks like.

Life isn't easy. Love isn't easy. Parenthood isn't easy. But it is all worth the pain, and worth choosing every day—even when the choice seems impossible.

I didn't think I could love this way. But God did. He gives me the strength and courage to love with everything I have.

Now I'm bringing a man into our lives—one who already loves my sons. It is both joyous and bittersweet. Once again, I am letting my sons be loved. I hoped one day my boys would know more than divorce. Now they will, with even more love.

And this is the greatest gift I could ever give my children: love.

Katie Weber is creator and writer of *Lovely in the Dark* blog. She is a mom and wife, living and loving her second chance after divorce.

My Path to Motherhood Didn't Look like I Planned

CHRISTINE JUDY

"I have a doctor's appointment," I say quietly as I give yet another notice of an upcoming absence to my boss. In this season, I see my reproductive endocrinologist twice a week every week, and the time away from the office has really added up over the last few months. If I'm honest, it's been adding up over the last few years.

I had hoped it would be easier, this journey to motherhood. My story doesn't look the way I thought it would.

If I'm not careful, I catch myself falling into the spiral of envy when I see surprise pregnancy announcements and hear about gender-reveal parties. The innocent, naive excitement strikes the aching chords of my heart. Oh, what I would give to have that kind of freedom in my soul.

Rather than daydreaming about what our children might look like, my husband and I approach each scan, appointment, and blood draw with apprehension. We know too much. Positive pregnancy tests don't send us into a celebratory dance, because we've seen those pink lines fade.

Our vacation plans revolve around when the next embryo transfer will be and how many medications I'll be on. This process has matured us, aged us. We're different now than when we started.

Instead of spending romantic nights with my husband, we have less than romantic mornings in the kitchen as we mix vials of medication and load syringes so my dearly beloved can stick another long needle into my caboose.

It isn't our first trip around this particular block. We have a miracle toddler at home, and we knew we were engaging in an uphill battle when we decided to try to give her a sibling.

After several diagnostic procedures, an egg retrieval surgery, genetic testing on our embryos, and a successful transfer, we are one step closer to bringing home another miracle. It is not lost on me that many couples never reach this point, and I have a lot to be grateful for. But amid my relief, I am also struck with unparalleled grief.

We have created more embryos than we will be able to bring home.

There are no guarantees when you're going through the in vitro fertilization process. With each stage—fertilization, blastocysts, embryos, genetic testing, cryopreservation, and thawing—approximately 40 to 60 percent will be lost. Our embryo babies, or embabies, beat the odds.

God must have been thinking about another mama too while He was answering our prayers. One day I will look another mother in the eye and entrust her with my heart through embryo adoption. She will love and raise my embabies, and they will call her "Mama."

For the love they'll have, I am thankful. I know how much this woman will love, desire, and care for these babies, because I, too, have fought this uphill battle of infertility and pregnancy loss, and her journey to motherhood hasn't been easy either.

I pray for her, this woman who will raise our babies, and I know she's walking through the trenches in a parallel world right now. I feel like I know her already, because only someone who has walked this road can truly understand the depth of this particular kind of hurt. Appointments, disappointments, broken dreams, fear, and hope create the rhythm of our hearts in this season. I hope she will know how much I love her for raising our babies and giving them life outside the frozen canisters they sit in now, waiting.

I pray our embabies know how much I love them too. Giving them to their future mama will be the hardest thing I'll ever do. I want them to feel chosen, wanted, and known all the days of their lives. I pray they will understand our decision one day, and I pray they'll never feel inferior to their genetic siblings who live under our roof. If we could raise them all, we would.

Embryo adoption is a beautiful thing, but for every rejoicing mama-to-be, there's a grieving mama hoping and praying her babies are safe and loved and that she'll be lucky enough to meet them one day.

My journey to motherhood hasn't been easy, but I never imagined I would have to say goodbye to part of my heart. Our embabies will always have two mamas: the one who gave them life and the one who gave them a future.

They may not be in my house, but they will be forever in my heart.

Christine Judy started the blog *The Judy Journey* to document her journey through infertility, IVF, and embryo adoption.

Me before Motherhood

ALIETTE SILVA

✕

I promise I do not always look like this, I think as I run into an old friend at the store.

My hair is a mess, and I'm wearing leggings for the fourth time this week.

My old friend is perfectly put together as she describes her life in the big city. She is not responsible for anyone but herself.

For a second, I feel envious of that kind of freedom. Motherhood sometimes feels like a trail of broken dreams.

Before we became mothers, we were *I.*

I want to study at a faraway university.

I want to work in Los Angeles.

I want to live as a single woman in a New York City apartment.

I want to travel the world and accomplish my goals.

Our dreams were varied, and our goals were lofty.

Remember how it felt when you were a child and you said, "When I grow up, I want to be . . ."? Being a mother may have been part of the answer, but it usually wasn't the whole answer.

Motherhood can feel like a permanent pause on everything we were before we became "Mom." It can feel constricting and suffocating, like our time is no longer our own.

I used to love extended sweat sessions at the gym—time to work on just me, with yoga and long walks. I enjoyed connecting and laughing with my best girlfriends: "I'll have a margarita, please!" as we ate nachos and shared stories.

Before I was a mother, I didn't have to answer to anyone.

Now all my decisions center on what's best for my children. My independence is entangled with them, and their needs come first.

Getting up in the morning and doing what I want is no longer an option. My brain never shuts off when it comes to my children. "I'll have a margarita, please, and a side of constant obligation" is a mother's motto.

I sometimes struggle to remember who I was before motherhood. Sometimes, for fleeting moments, I want my life before I had children back. At first, guilt consumes me, and I feel egotistical and self-serving. I have two healthy children, and I am incredibly blessed.

But I remind myself it's okay to be a woman with dreams. It's okay to crave "me time." It's okay to worry I've lost a bit of myself in motherhood.

Then I consider the life I have now. It waits for me to make new memories with my children. It invites me to shift my dreams but not abandon them.

My life is fulfilling, despite how different it looks from what I'd imagined. My mornings consist of "Mama, I love you. Can you snuggle with me for a minute?" My body moves to impromptu dance parties in the kitchen. I am paid with an intangible salary of homemade cards and fingers sticky from baking treats. Each December my world is lit up by children whose eyes twinkle underneath a Christmas tree. My soul is filled with the laughter of my children, and they are gifts that keep on giving.

Before I was a mother, I was all about myself. In service to my children, I have learned our souls are nourished when we serve others.

This doesn't mean I've given up on my dreams. They have simply changed.

I'm still learning how to incorporate my personal dreams into my motherhood journey. It's a delicate balance between my independence and my children's needs.

In Spanish, we have a saying: *No puedes vivir de sueños. You can't live in your dreams, because you have to live in the now.*

You can still pursue your dreams, perhaps with a few detours along the way. Embracing motherhood only makes the view that much more breathtaking.

Aliette Silva is a bilingual freelance writer. When she's not writing, you can find her chasing sleep, her children, or a good Cuban sandwich.

Running from God

MELISSA NEEB

God sees me, my whole life. Even when I'm running from Him.

He sees me when I'm running from the church where I don't feel seen. The one I attend every week as a child and am allowed to miss only if I have a fever or am throwing up. I feel all wrong here in my Sunday best, with shiny shoes and a shiny smile plastered on. The church of my youth is a place for perfection, and even with a clean face, my insides are dirty. I can't show my brokenness here. I have to stuff the shards of brokenness into my little dress pockets and pull them out only in the safety of my bedroom.

So I run from God.

God sees me in the bar I land in at twenty-one, when I meet the man who eventually becomes my husband. We are drawn to each other like moths to a wildfire, and we quickly become consumed in both the best and worst possible ways. It is toxic and intoxicating, adventurous and reckless. Alcohol makes us brave in the wrong things and cowards when it matters most. It makes us dangerous to ourselves and to each other.

Six months later, I am curled up like a question mark on the cold bathroom floor, eyes squeezed shut, a positive pregnancy test balancing precariously on the edge of the bathroom sink and on the edge of my sanity.

I am fumbling at the door to my thoughts; they have locked me in. I am living the nightmare where I'm in an abandoned building with rooms and corridors that keep expanding and changing and there are countless doors to nowhere. There is no way out.

Several people suggest abortion or adoption. I can't fathom either. This baby is a part of me. We dream together, hiccup together, exist in this new and uncertain landscape together. My plans rip to shreds and scatter like confetti in the brisk September breeze. New blueprints are drawn, but I have not handed over the pen. These plans are my design. Things will be different now, I tell myself. Better.

I continue running from God.

God sees me as my life unravels. I am married now, and my husband's drinking has gone from habitual to obsessive. When we take our toddler to the playground, he brings a six-pack along. He drinks for every occasion, and also when there is none. His glass has no bottom.

After our second child is born, he has a botched surgery and begins using hard drugs.

It's 2:30 a.m., and I am nursing my daughter while soothing my son's night terrors. I am caring for our children alone. Afterward, I slide the blinds open, willing my husband to come home. He left to get cigarettes hours earlier. I am waiting in vain. He doesn't appear until morning, ready excuse in hand.

I am married to my best friend. I am married to a stranger.

His behavior becomes more and more erratic. His moods are wild, and I am tethered to them, gripping tightly as I am lurched back and forth in the cyclone of him. I would do anything, become anyone, change everything for him to get sober.

But nothing I do changes my reality.

God sees me as I love our two beautiful babies in the midst of the chaos I can see no end to. He sees me angry and drowning in resentment because I am living a life I never imagined—one where I am consumed with the behaviors of someone I have no control over. I lose myself completely trying to fix what is not mine to fix.

I am not on speaking terms with God. I don't know how to pray. I feel abandoned, forgotten. If He is here in the nitty-gritty details, I can't see Him. I am bitterly angry at Him for not changing my circumstances. For not healing my husband's disease. For not redeeming the agony that feels unbearable, insurmountable.

God sees me in all the years that go by. In the cycles of my husband's sobriety and relapses, in all the support groups we attend, in the devastation of past hurts and long-held grudges, in the treatments, the DUI, the car accidents, the jail stints.

He sees me white-knuckling our secrets, desperate to present our okay-ness to the world even though we scatter like puzzle pieces across the floor once our front door clicks shut.

God sees me on the bedroom floor at the moment of my rock bottom, in utter despair. I am buried under the rubble of my hopelessness. I barely have the strength to reach out to Him, to beg for oxygen, to plead to be pulled out of this pit.

I am unable to run any longer. I can't live like this anymore. It is my moment of complete surrender.

God weaves my clammy fingers through His graceful ones and gently whispers, "Girl, are you ready to stop running?"

I am. I have come to the end of myself. The end of thinking I know what's best. The end of thinking I can do it better. The end of bloody, chewed-up, clawing-for-control fingernails. My body physically can't go any farther, and my mind isn't going to make me anymore.

God sees me in every moment of my life. He has exquisitely, painstakingly mapped my roads to converge right here.

The only choice is Him. I no longer have anything to run from. The darkness has no hold on me.

God sees it all. He sees me. My rock bottom becomes the foundation for my brand-new life.

God and I are off and running. We are going to finish this journey. Together.

Melissa Neeb is a Jesus-loving wife, mom, and blogger for *Faith in the Mess* and *Never Empty Nest*. Follow along on social media!

Motherhood Terrified Me

JESSIKA SANDERS

As a little girl, I played house. But unlike the other girls, I didn't dream of being a mommy with a bunch of babies.

In middle school, I doodled the names of boys and planned my future playing MASH. But unlike my friends, I was okay landing on zero children.

In high school I occasionally babysat for extra cash. But unlike my peers, I didn't fall in love with the kids.

In my twenties, I had multiple relationships. But unlike some women my age, I didn't have any plans to settle down or conceive children.

Motherhood terrified me because I felt like I wasn't cut out for it.

I felt like the cards were stacked against me.

I felt completely ill equipped.

I felt sure I would fail.

Was I capable of unconditional love? Could I put the needs of others ahead of my own? Was it possible for my wanderlust-filled soul to be tied down, connected to, and responsible for other humans for my entire life?

I knew my dysfunctional childhood was at the root of these doubts and fears. My lack of positive examples left me certain motherhood would be a risk—a mistake, even.

But regardless of upbringing, society expects women to fit into the mold of getting married and having kids. The expectation finds its way into our lives from a young age, even through childhood rhymes: "First comes love, then comes marriage, then comes so-and-so with the baby carriage."

If I'm honest, my people-pleasing nature never stood a chance against culture. Without much discretion and on a whim, I got married. Within a year, I was pregnant. I naively hoped I would do less damage than my parents had. After experiencing all the negative examples, I hoped I'd have a foolproof framework for what not to do.

Not so much.

Despite my good intentions, I followed in my parents' footsteps. I rushed into marriage, and an abusive one, at that. When my husband confessed infidelity, I decided on divorce. Although the decision was mine, it still stung. The guilt was almost unbearable, because I knew firsthand the lifelong pain this would inflict on my children. My heart broke at the thought of robbing them of the possibility of a happy nuclear family.

My doubts and fears had manifested into reality, and I felt like a complete failure.

However, four years into motherhood, and in the midst of my failed attempt at happily ever after, I found healing, clarity, and direction. It wasn't from on-the-job-training, from a self-help book, or from a Facebook post. I found this healing when I met God.

God was the Light in that dark season of marriage and motherhood. As I spent time with Him, studying His Word and learning His character, it changed me. Though I was weighed down by all my baggage, God gently picked me up and took me in. He accepted me into His family, and I experienced love like never before.

It's funny—I expected to learn how to parent from my mother, but God's love for me ended up being the exact model I needed. His unconditional, sacrificial, steadfast love transformed my heart. The walls of fear and doubt I'd built around me came crumbling down. And with the walls removed and the Light pouring in, I saw motherhood in a new way, with a new perspective.

Years later, remarried and with another baby in tow, I no longer believe the lies. Instead, I remind myself of His truth—a truth that applies to you, too.

God's grace is sufficient. With Him, we can be the mothers He has called us to be. The love God bestows on us equips and enables us to love our children well. While we fall short, He never fails—and neither does His love.

I used to be terrified of motherhood, but then I met God.

Jessika Sanders is a wife, mother, writer, and founder of Praying Through ministries, a non-profit that serves families journeying through the NICU, PICU, and child loss.

I Pray the World Doesn't Change Her

JENNY ALBERS

✕

My daughter is the same age I was when the opinions of others began to take hold and shape me into someone I wasn't. I walked into school one day wholly myself and came out as someone else.

Now that I'm on the verge of parenting a middle-school girl, I'm acutely aware of how hard those in-between years are, and I find myself praying the world doesn't change her like it did me.

I was in fifth grade when I fearlessly arrived at school wearing a straight-off-the-rack outfit I'd proudly used my own money to buy. It was a pink sweatsuit adorned with large, plastic, multicolored gemstones. As a ten-year-old in the early nineties, it was the most glorious thing I'd ever seen.

But then it happened. A classmate I'll lovingly call Mean Girl said something to me I've never forgotten: "Ew. Pink is so ugly. I wouldn't be caught dead wearing that." She looked me up and down, scoffed, and turned away with a look of disgust on her face.

I shrank, willing myself to become invisible.

It was the first time I remember confusing an opinion about me for truth, the first time I mistakenly assumed I had a responsibility to meet someone else's superficial standards.

I hid that outfit at the bottom of a pile in my bedroom closet, attempting to forget about it. But I never did. Because that outfit was—and still is—100 percent me. Pink and jewels are still two of my favorites. But for too long, I buried those parts of myself because of that girl's opinion. It was the beginning of a years-long stretch when I constantly tried to shape myself into who I thought other people wanted me to be.

I'm probably not supposed to admit this, but years later, when an ultrasound revealed I would soon be mothering a baby girl, I was disappointed. I had hoped for a boy, prayed for a boy. Not because I had anything against girls, but because I felt unequipped to raise one. Scenes from that day in fifth grade flashed through my mind. Mean Girl's disdain still haunted me, as did the years I'd spent trying to please her.

How would I protect my daughter from whatever version of Mean Girl she would inevitably face? How would I keep her from forcing herself to fit into a mold that wasn't made for her? How would I help her embrace her best traits even when she was met with disapproval?

In a decade of parenting, I haven't yet come up with answers. But as we navigate the confusing growing-up-but-not-yet-grown-up years, I hope I've instilled the truth in my daughter—that God made a mold just for her and she'll never fit another one as beautifully as she fits her own.

I don't imagine there will be any plastic gemstone–encrusted sweatsuits in her future. But my daughter does have a distinct take on fashion and on life. *When will it happen?* I wonder. *Who will voice disapproval of her style? Who will mock her natural abilities and interests? Who will look at her or speak to her in a way that convinces her she needs to bury parts of herself?*

I hope her personal style never finds itself at the bottom of a pile in her bedroom closet. I hope her perspective on life doesn't change solely based on someone's perception of her. I hope my habit of complimenting her uniqueness will cause her to wear and be her true self, even when someone rejects her.

Even though raising a girl wasn't part of my plan, I'm grateful it was part of God's. I can't believe I ever prayed for my daughter to be someone else, because the only thing I want now is for her to be exactly who she is—always.

But I know the world has plans too. It has its own standards of beauty and worth. It will seek to change my girl. To break her spirit. To squash her confidence. To compel her to betray her gifts and interests. To seduce her into denying herself for the sake of fitting into someone else's mold.

And when that happens, I pray she does what I didn't do. I hope she won't hush the opinions about who she should be and will instead internalize the truth of who God says she already is. Wonderfully created. Worthy. Loved more than she can fathom.

I pray I'm raising her in such a way that she won't give the world power to change her. And that when it tries to shape her into someone else, she'll boldly reject its efforts and revel in the mold made exclusively for her, the shape she wears best: herself.

Jenny Albers is the author of *Courageously Expecting: 30 Days of Encouragement During Pregnancy After Loss.*

The Story
I Didn't Want to Tell

JENNIFER THOMPSON

✕

Once upon a time, there was a girl who lived in a small Indiana town. She attended a school where everybody knew everybody's name, and it was there she met her Prince Charming. At seventeen, she fell in love with this boy, and their beautiful romance began.

But as with most stories, my love story was not all bliss.

At nineteen, as I was walking home from class at the university, I realized it had been a while since my last period. I made a detour to the local pharmacy and strolled to my boyfriend's house to take the test.

And as the two lines appeared, tears formed in my eyes. This would be the greatest moment of some people's lives, but for me, it felt suffocating and scary. This was not a part of my plan. I walked slowly out of the room, test in hand.

What would I do?

What *should* I do?

I felt so confused. I felt trapped in a hopeless situation. I had dreams and plans for my life. There was an order to my plans, and having a baby felt impossible then. How would I finish school? Where would I live? What would I do? I felt too young to get married and definitely too young and irresponsible to care for a baby.

But at the same time, I knew in my heart life was growing inside of me. I knew this was a product of my boyfriend's and my love, and once I held this child in my arms, my heart would forever belong to him or her.

During those days of indecision and confusion, there were many sleepless nights when I would lie in bed for hours with my hands resting softly on my abdomen, painfully aware of what was happening inside. During those nights, my pillow was covered in mascara stains and soaked with tears.

This is the part of the story I once struggled to tell. This is the part I kept guarded and locked away in my heart, held captive by the fear of what others would think of me if they discovered this truth.

At nineteen, I chose to have an abortion.

After making the decision, my boyfriend and I went to a church down the road and asked to meet with the pastor. I had to know: Would we be forgiven? Was this an unforgivable sin? Would God ever love me again?

The pastor assured me there was nothing I could do to take away God's love, but I wasn't sure I believed that.

How could I take the life of my child and still be loved by God?

But what I've learned over the years is God loved me then and He loves me now. The words the pastor spoke over me that day in the small church room that smelled of must and old books were true. God's love isn't based on what I did or didn't do. It isn't based on my choices. It simply is—now and always.

Even in our darkest moments.

Even in our most desperate times.

Even in those times we wish we could take it back and do it over.

He is still there, loving us through it all.

God knew all along what choice I would make, but He still pursued me. He still loved me. I just needed to accept that love.

That's why I tell the story I once tried so hard to hide. That's why these words are here for you to read. Because maybe, just maybe, this is a part of your story too.

Maybe you need to know you are forgiven for that choice you made. Maybe you need to know God can take what's broken and make it new. The hurt. The shame. The past mistakes. All of it.

Years later, that boyfriend and I got married, and have since had four children.

I've often wondered how we will tell them this part of our story. How do we let them know they have a brother or sister in heaven because of a choice we made long ago?

I used to worry God would punish me or that I wouldn't be a good mom because of this choice. I wondered how someone who took the life of her child could be considered a good mom. I used to think I didn't have a right to grieve or to feel this pain because it was a product of my choice.

After years of healing, I know that's not true. They were lies I held on to that I've since been released from.

God would not withhold His love from me because of my choice. That's not who He is. This choice has no bearing on if I am a good mom to my children now.

I still need to grieve my loss. I will forever miss my baby, and I will always wonder. I wonder if we would have had a boy or a girl. I wonder what he or she would be like today.

I will never hold or kiss or hug my child. I will never wipe away their tears or kiss their boo-boo. I will never get to tell them "I love you" or "I'm sorry." At least not here on earth.

But I believe I will be united with my child one day. I believe I will hold that child in my arms and say all the things I long to say.

While I wish my story were different, it's mine. And I've seen how God has redeemed my pain and used it for His glory.

If this is part of your story too, I pray you will accept the forgiveness you've been offered and know you, too, are fully loved.

Jennifer Thompson writes at *Truly Yours, Jen* and hopes her words will feel warm, encouraging, inviting, and honest, like receiving a letter from a friend.

PART 8

SO GOD MADE A MOTHER

unforgettable

✕

"The days are long, but
the years are short," they say.
And they're right—but what
they forget to mention is that
the heart remembers it all.

HER VIEW FROM HOME

The Dishes

✕

When I was twenty-three years old, my mother bought me a set of discount dishes. She told me it was the last box on the shelf and she had to "fight off another lady for them."

I don't think Mom threw any punches, but the women in my family do have a way of getting what we want. I'm sure she furrowed an aggressive eyebrow and gave that stranger a stare-down before grabbing the half-priced box.

These dishes weren't extravagant (do they sell fancy dishes at discount stores?), but they were beautiful and sturdy. The mugs were big enough to hold two cups of coffee—or a bowl of cereal, my food of choice. A gallon of milk and a box of cereal can go a long way for a broke newlywed.

The bowls matched the mugs, each adorned with three pink and green flowers. And they could hold a quart of ice cream, which I discovered once during my stressful early years working in TV.

These dishes traveled with my husband and me to our first apartment in Houston. Each time I used the mugs, I thought of home and my mom. It was a welcome comfort during a lonely season.

They've been thrown into boxes and moved four more times since then and are quickly approaching seventeen years of age. Told you they're sturdy.

Although the set is no longer complete, a few mugs and bowls still sit in our

209

cupboards. Fortunately, I've been able to swap cereal for pasta, but unfortunately, I'm no longer able to eat a quart of ice cream in one sitting (although I think my girls have already accomplished this task).

It's still my favorite set of dishes. But my husband is curious.

"Les," he said to me once, "when we move into our new home, we should replace all our pots and pans and dishes."

Here's something you need to know about my husband and me: we're at a point financially where we can afford new pots and pans and dishes. But we both grew up in homes where fancy dishes were a luxury, so it seems rather strange to put money into something that's simply a tool for eating food.

"I agree, we need new pots and pans," I told him. "But I'm keeping the mugs. And the bowls."

He gave me a look. I gave him a look.

Here's something you should also know about me: I like to keep things. It could be because my grandmother used to wash and reuse disposable bags, a product of growing up during the Depression, and my father keeps every piece of scrap metal and farm equipment he's ever owned, a product of growing up with a mother and father who didn't have much money.

And the cycle continues.

But I don't keep baggies or farm equipment. I just keep bowls and mugs my mama aggressively fought for so her baby could use something other than her hands to eat cereal.

It's funny—these dishes sold only because a half-price sticker was on the box. Now they're priceless, because the heart never forgets.

It's one of the special things about moms, isn't it? Our love leaves a mark, and motherhood leaves a mark on us. You'll see why in these next few stories.

Crying in the Cereal Aisle Again

MELISSA FENTON

It didn't really hit me until the cereal aisle, where I found myself ugly-crying in front of oversized, bright yellow boxes of Cheerios.

I'd been there years before, of course, just like every other exhausted mother of babies and toddlers who inevitably finds herself having a breakdown in the most public of places. I was intimately familiar with what was happening. My head pounded, my eyes misted, my breath grew irregular, and my logical brain begged the question, *How did I get here?* But my heart? Well, it simply ached.

It ached because those little ones who used to bring me to my knees are now grown and moving out. I was crying now not because my days were filled with mindless and exhausting tasks like sweeping cereal off the floor and washing sippy cup valves but because that kid who loved Cheerios just left for college and I no longer needed them on my grocery list.

When I saw that familiar yellow box, the realization hit me that although a mindless task had been removed from my to-do list (and I probably should have cheered the fact my grocery bill would drop significantly), it only reminded me of that tiny child gripping handfuls of tiny Os and a babyhood that turned into childhood that turned into adolescence and had now become a season I was no longer a primary part of. He had moved out.

Strangely enough, it happened just like those older moms said it would years ago, when I was in the weeds of taking care of four little ones and constantly hearing, "You're going to miss this one day, because it really does go by so fast."

They were correct, but there was something more crucial and affirming they neglected to tell me: kids growing up and moving away is what's *supposed* to happen. It's the natural course of things, and when we start to look at this process of growing up with gratitude and pride instead of mourning, it's much easier to handle.

Is it hard when our babies leave? Of course it is, in much the same way bringing home your first newborn left you feeling lost and unsure of what it meant to be a good mother, the way every day brought with it new emotions and doubts. So, too, is the transition when those babies begin their adult lives.

Since the incident in the cereal aisle, I've sent another child off to college, and I'm a few months shy of sending off number three. I can say with complete confidence my days of sobbing in the breakfast aisle are a thing of the past. As frustrating and infuriating as the phrase "new normal" can be, it's also the plain truth. While I once felt miserably somber when walking into a clean, empty bedroom, I now feel relief. It's not because that child represented a burden now absent; it's because having empty bedrooms is the goal of parenting. Letting go of kids and releasing them into the world to start their own journey means I successfully raised humans whose purpose is outside my home.

Parenting isn't meant to be days of endless sadness, longing for an eternal childhood. It's days filled with the honor and privilege of watching your children fulfill their purpose—which is inherently your purpose, and has been God's purpose all along.

Does that mean you're not permitted to grieve a bit for those simple days spent with little ones underfoot? Of course not! As a matter of fact, you'll eventually find yourself looking back with unexplainable fondness at toddler tantrums, experiencing an insatiable desire to smell the heads of babies, and longing for a time when problems could be solved with a nap and a lollipop.

But in exchange, you'll see adult children who are the ultimate manifestation of all the hard work you put in. And you'll be able to truly enjoy them. Going from their mom to their mentor to their friend is a reward you get to savor for decades.

Besides, just about the time an empty house starts to let the melancholy creep in, something even more wonderful happens. They're called grandchildren . . . who will definitely need Cheerios. Amen.

Melissa Fenton, writer and mother of four sons, has words all over the Internet, but her best work is on the dinner table.

Dear Mother-In-Law, I Wish You Were Still Here

ELLIE HUNJA

✕

To my mother-in-law:

Can I be honest? I was terrified to meet you.

You were everyone's favorite. Each of my future husband's college friends seemed to have a sweet story about your visits to campus, how your youthful spirit and contagious laugh made you fit right in.

I heard the joy and ease in their stories, and I wondered how our interactions would have compared. After all, I was a white American girl coming to Kenya to meet you, then start a life with your youngest child thousands of miles from where you raised him.

Your amazing son and I were in our mid-twenties, still figuring out our own identities and the dynamics of a marriage. But I wanted to seem sure of myself. I assumed you had an image of your ideal daughter-in-law in mind—and I wasn't it. I wanted to show you I was good enough for your son, despite not coming from your tribe, your country, or even your continent.

Your embrace instantly melted my fears. You were kindhearted, effervescent, and hilarious, just like everyone said. You loved me like a daughter. But our relationship wasn't without strain. You were invested in our decisions, anxious about the choices we made, and shared your opinions freely. Hunja and I would have long conversations in tense, hushed tones, trying to figure out how we could best honor you while still setting healthy boundaries.

The bottom line was that you cared. A lot. At times that felt overbearing, as if we had to carry your worries along with our own.

Now that I've grown into motherhood and know the fierce, protective love a mother has for her children, I understand you better. But back then, we so desperately wanted to be seen as grown, capable, and competent.

Then, when our marriage and our firstborn were both still in the toddler stage, you received a diagnosis: cancer. You fought for two years, but as our second child grew in my belly, we said our goodbyes and you transitioned to glory.

Today I would give anything to be navigating the growing pains of our relationship instead of living another year without you. I try not to carry any regrets, but I wish we'd had time to get past the formalities and pressures and expectations of what it means to be a Kikuyu daughter-in-law. I wish we'd had time for our love to grow.

You were an empowered woman who took up space and spoke her mind. You never shrank yourself for anyone. You honored tradition but still blazed your own path, pursuing an education and a career that brought you great fulfillment as you raised two sons.

You showed my husband what a fully realized woman looks like and, in so doing, raised a son who doesn't expect women to shrink in his presence. I'm . . . well, I'm a *lot*, and I can confidently say you prepared him for me. Your son is an introvert and a peacemaker at heart, but he is not intimidated by my boisterous personality. He loves every part of me, and his calming presence is a safe haven for me to bring my full self.

You gave me my life's greatest gift: the best partner I could have asked for. I wish I'd had the chance to truly express my gratitude, mature past the growing pains, and allow our relationship to slip into a comfortable ease. There is so much more you and I would have become, so much beauty that could have unfolded, if only we'd had the chance.

But I know you'd remind me life is too short to hold on to regrets. So in your absence, I try to embrace your wisdom. You always kept an eternal perspective, with a clear picture of the glory and joy that await us in heaven. I try to live in light of that truth. I reflect on how you faced unimaginable pain and difficulty with honesty, courage, and faith in God's sovereignty. Your example strengthens me when my own faith feels lacking.

And when a new bride asks me for advice on in-laws, I smile knowingly and swallow the lump in my throat. After extolling boundaries and communication and marital unity, I tell her the most important thing: whatever isn't essential to the health of your marriage, lay it down. Lay it down. Lay it down.

I wish I had laid more down. I wish I'd spent less time drawing boundaries and more time deepening my own sense of self so I could let the small things roll off my back.

Dear mother-in-law, I wish I'd spent more time embracing you—all of you, the gifts and the flaws and everything in-between. You were a mom, after all, trying to do the best you could. Just like I am.

Ellie Hunja pursues joy, authenticity, and mental health in motherhood. Visit her self-titled blog and Instagram (@elliehunja) for reflections on parenting, faith, and embracing autism.

The Little Blue Stool

LISA LESHAW

It was time to tackle a toothbrushing routine for the two-year-old. To herald its arrival, Grandpa built his grandson, "Mush," a little blue stool to stand on.

Swishing, long-distance spitting, and making toothpaste mustaches became joy-filled daily rituals for my little boy. The little blue stool remained front and center next to the sink for nearly a year, but it soon graduated to a much more important role: the perfect-sized step-up to a big boy bed.

Every evening, like clockwork, Mush retrieved the stool and placed it beside his bed for our nighttime ritual.

"Mama, sit, pease," he'd say as he patted the stool before climbing into bed.

I needed no encouragement. I took that seat of honor, the best one in the house, and hoped no one would disturb this precious time, forever. Dirty dishes and overflowing laundry baskets be darned. Nothing would budge me from this royal throne.

Mush would scoot to the edge of the bed, and I'd rest my head right next to his. I'd smell his strawberry shampoo and grape juice breath. If I could have, I'd have devoured his goodness for breakfast, lunch, supper, and all the hours in between.

The rule was one book before bedtime, but Mush and I, in an easy collaboration of hearts, always read two (or maybe three). Sometimes I deliberately lost count.

Goodnight Moon was always our first choice. Even if we read it four times, we only counted it as one. Nose rubs and kisses were snuck in after every stanza.

"Goodnight room." Kisses. Nose rubs.

"Goodnight moon." Nose rubs. Kisses.

"Goodnight cow jumping over the moon." Sloppy kisses. Noisy laughter.

Oh, don't let this ever end.

Every effort to create calm and induce sleepiness was undone each time we read *Chicka Chicka Boom Boom*, because when we got to the "boom boom" part, we made the walls quake with our booming voices.

More laughter. Nearly falling-out-of-bed laughter.

When I lowered my voice to a soft whisper, it signaled the beginning of our prayers, hand holding, hugging, and closed eyes.

We thanked God for everything. It took a while. We knew He'd love our list.

From the baby birds to the marshmallow clouds. From Grandma Bea to the mail lady. From bubble baths to sidewalk chalk.

Our bedtime ritual was the highlight of my day. Even my crabbiest, crankiest, "not so happy with myself" days.

Even when I didn't think I could muster enough mama patience for a quality bedtime routine, Mush made me feel like I could, and I did.

At the start of third grade, Mush relegated the little blue stool to his closet and took it out every evening at 7:30.

Then one night in August, the stool wasn't there. I figured Mush must have gotten distracted or lost focus or fallen asleep or forgotten the time. I grabbed the stool from the closet and took my favorite seat.

Now Mush read to me. I lay my head on his pillow as we followed the adventures of Tom Sawyer and his friend Huck, learned valuable life lessons from a giving tree, and giggled at how Tigger bounced through life with Pooh.

When I got upstairs the next night, he'd already fallen asleep—before he had time to take out the little blue stool. He must have been exhausted.

I kissed his cheek and covered him up to his chin. I quietly recited *Guess How Much I Love You?*

On the third night, I peeked into his room before heading in. The stool wasn't there. He was reading to himself.

And I knew. What I didn't want to know. What I already knew.

He'd outgrown our ritual. Where is it written that bedtime rituals are to be given up without notice? Without any form of preparation? I wasn't ready.

I had no idea how to conduct myself. Should I walk in and ignore the elephant in the room? It was my elephant, not his.

I went to the bathroom and sat on the floor to put myself back together like Humpty Dumpty. The same Humpty Dumpty from the first nursery rhyme I read to Mush as a baby.

I sucked in air and washed my face with cold water. Then I walked into his room with a giant smile.

"Hi, Bud. Whatcha reading?"

And that's when we moved on to another chapter.

It wasn't what I wanted, but somewhere deep in my core, I knew it was a good thing.

I knew I should be proud of his growth, his independence.

Oh, I was proud—just not ready. But if I made him wait for me, he would be held captive by *my* needs, not his.

And so our bedtime routine was reduced to a few hair tousles and quick pecks on the cheek. We headed to newer adventures, greater milestones. Grander hopes, loftier dreams. Some together, some apart.

One night, many years later, Mush called down for a glass of water. I'd been home with the flu for a few days, so his dad offered to bring it to him, but I was headed up anyway. With water and a few vanilla wafers in hand, I turned the corner into his room.

The little blue stool was sitting by the side of the bed.

"I know you're tired, Mama. You can rest while I read you a story."

And at that moment, everything was right with the world.

Goodnight, moon.

Lisa Leshaw believes that through rich storytelling we discover just how alike we truly are and how much we need one another's embrace to thrive.

Tell the Story of
Your Imperfect Family

KATHY GLOW

×

I don't have many professional photographs of my family. I always knew I *should* get them taken; I just didn't want to. I aspired to document perfectly crafted memories of every age and stage of my children's lives, but for the past seventeen years, it hasn't worked out quite like that.

I had four chaotic boys who would not sit down, hold still, keep clean, smile naturally, or look at the camera at the same time. Every photo session left me sweating, disheveled, and totally disappointed in the results.

Maybe not *totally* disappointed, but the pictures revealed stories I wasn't willing to tell. They showed I was a failure as a mother, I didn't dress my kids in adorable clothing, and I couldn't discipline them to sit still. I eventually gave up on having a professional photo taken at all.

When my twins were five years old, one was diagnosed with terminal brain cancer. In addition to feeling shock, I also felt regret over not trying harder to capture those "ages and stages" photographs. Time with my son was running out, and I wouldn't have pictures to remember him by.

We rushed to a professional photographer and had family photos taken. Of course, I picked them apart—our outfits were thrown together, the boys' shoes were scuffed, and I could see the droopiness in Joey's eyes and smile, caused by his ongoing seizures. Regardless, I chose the best photo as our holiday card: a black-and-white shot of the six of us wrapped in a hug.

To an outsider, the photo told the story of a picture-perfect family. Everyone who received our card that year, though, knew the real, heartbreaking story. They knew about Joey's diagnosis and our family's sadness and pain.

By the following Christmas, Joey had died, and I was unexpectedly pregnant. I didn't feel like sending out a picture card at all. I didn't want one that was missing Joey, and I wasn't ready to share about our new baby with anyone.

As time went on, the baby grew into a toddler and our grief softened. Then, through a bid at a charity event, we acquired a portrait session with a professional photographer. My old fears of disastrous photos crept in, as well as the sadness of not having Joey in the picture. But I knew if I didn't at least attempt to keep taking family photos, I would regret it. I told our story to the photographer, and she shared an idea with us. She had a way to include Joey.

The results were amazing. Incredibly, we were all looking at the camera with beautiful smiles on our faces. One of our sons was holding a framed black-and-white picture of Joey from the photo session after his diagnosis. This picture told of a family missing one of their own but able to move forward in healing and hope. That picture still hangs in my house, our boys frozen in time as young children.

Despite that successful photo, I remained hesitant to have family pictures taken. While I was once nagged by the fear of imperfection, my hesitancy now was about the passage of time. I didn't want a visual reminder of the other boys as teenagers while Joey was forever age six.

By Christmas 2020, the pandemic was in full swing, and we spent the entire holiday break in our pajamas. On New Year's Eve, I realized I had forgotten to mark that Christmas with a picture. I made my sons change out of their pajamas and don something presentable, and I assembled everyone by the tree. Several attempts later, I finally had a photo I felt was Facebook-worthy.

I posted it, along with the story of how it wasn't the perfect family picture and how it was a week late in coming. I talked of having to beg my teenagers to put on decent clothing after spending the past week unshowered and in pajamas. I even mentioned the gas bombs dropped on siblings during the taking of the picture. But I also told the truth about how we'd laughed until we'd cried while trying to get the snapshot just right.

Looking back on all my family photos, professional and candid, I realize they do, in fact, tell our story. They portray a young, happy couple who wanted a lot of children. They share the story of a little boy ravaged by cancer. They tell of a family that moved forward after loss and then welcomed an unexpected blessing. They reveal boys who are boys and a mom who tries her best while loving her children fiercely. They include scuffed shoes and wrinkled shirts and the empty space where our seventh man should be. They show everything that makes us the family we are.

I've finally realized I need to stop being afraid of the reality our pictures show and embrace their honesty instead. After all, this is our family, perfectly imperfect, just the way we are.

Kathy Glow, wife and boy mom, has written for websites, anthologies, and magazines. Her blog, *Kissing the Frog*, details life after all your dreams come true.

Defining Moments

MICHELLE KOCH

When I was a young adult, I worked a flexible outside-sales job. This made me the ideal candidate to accompany my grandparents to a medical appointment downtown. My grandma was very special to me, and I would have driven her across the country if she needed me to.

It wasn't a standard appointment. It was time to see if the cancer was back.

The youthful confidence that enabled me to navigate the traffic and large hospital evaporated when we sat in the exam room. There didn't seem to be enough space or oxygen, and I was suddenly a scared little girl. As the doctor delivered the dreaded news, I bit my tongue and squeezed my fingernails into my palms.

Over and over in my head, I told myself to be a grown-up. For the first time in my life, I needed to be strong for my grandparents, and falling apart wasn't going to help them. I watched them lock eyes with each other, and all I saw was fear. Fear of what was to come, fear of saying goodbye.

I felt it with every ounce of my being too. I didn't want my grandmother to suffer, and the thought of losing her broke my heart. But I couldn't let it show. I held in my breath and my tears for what felt like days, even though it was only hours. I'd wait until I was alone to fall apart.

Now, when I look back on that day, more than a decade after both of my grandparents left this earth, I don't focus on the fear. Instead, I remember the way my grandfather paused to smell the flowering crabapple trees that lined the sidewalk on the way into the hospital. We all knew what was likely about to happen, and the tension was thick in the air—but so was the scent of spring. It was a beautiful day, and the pink blossoms that covered the trees only last a short time. He knew that.

The defining moments of life often mark the ending of one season and the beginning of another. But too often we try to pivot into a new role or accept a new emptiness without pausing to mourn for what was. The pace of life doesn't allow us much time to miss who we once were or to look back on a time when we took the future for granted. We need to slow our pace to steady ourselves but instead are rushed forward long before we're steady on our feet.

What a shame that is, for if we're hurried into spring while our bones still hold a chill or if we're swept into summer when we're still too weak to emerge from the dirt, we'll never be able to be fully present in the beauty of today.

As a mom, I've learned this lesson in a profound way. I don't get to decide when my children are ready to move to the next stage, any more than I can force crabapple trees to blossom. The only thing I have control over is if I will take the time to breathe in the fragrance of the beauty of right now.

To everything there is a season. There are seasons to be savored and those that are simply to be survived. Life is bittersweet that way.

We live in a fast-paced world where holiday decór stocks store shelves before the back-to-school supplies run out. This leaves us with little chance to enjoy the here and now. No doubt my grandparents learned these lessons long before that day at the hospital. My grandpa stopped and pulled that flower-covered branch close to his weathered face because he knew waiting for the perfect time or a better day may not be in the cards.

In the days and months that followed that appointment, my grandparents cared for each other as best they could in sickness and in health, until death parted them. That is what matters.

And each spring as the trees bloom, I'm reminded each season is a gift—even the hard ones—and they're worth taking the time to memorize in your heart.

Michelle Koch is a middle-aged, young-at-heart storyteller, wife, and mom. She is a lifelong gratitude enthusiast; connect with her blog and socials at *One Grateful Girl.*

If God Calls Me Home

STACEY TADLOCK

Dear Husband,

I never thought I would sit down to write a letter like this—I am too young to write a letter like this. It's funny to say that because so often I look at myself in the mirror and ask you, "Babe, when did I get so old?" But here I am, realizing this is not old enough, not by a long shot.

I have so many thoughts circling in my head of things I need you to do if God calls me home. I hope after my medical test next week the news is great and you can simply tuck this letter away and we can continue dreaming of our golden years, when we'll hold hands on a porch swing. But if that time doesn't come for us, there is so much you need to know.

So often I tell people our marriage is fifty-fifty. But I've had to look hard at our family recently and wonder what it would look like if you were the only parent here. So many little things that make our life what it is come from me.

Like the overpriced hand soaps I buy every season—the girls love those soaps. They love picking out their favorite scents when I take them shopping. They *ooh* and *ahh* over the cute new bottle designs. You smile and say seventy-five-cent soap from the grocery store works just as well, but the girls will need the soap. It will remind them of me. Don't stop buying the fancy soap.

Our house is a home because I've made it warm and cozy. The wall hangings and framed pictures, the seasonal wreaths, the decorations for every holiday—that's all me, and the girls will need it. They'll need you to buy pumpkins and mums for fall. They'll need you to put out the holiday hand towels and all our Christmas knickknacks. They'll need our home to feel as welcoming as I've always made it.

Please remember to take pictures. Print them, buy frames, and hang them in our home. Don't let that stop with me. When they look back, they need to know their life didn't stop because mine did. They need to have memories captured. That means all their future smiles, giggles, and significant moments will be in your hands. You have to keep that going.

You will need to learn how to cook their favorite meals and how to book their hair appointments (always say no to bangs). You have to remember treats for teachers at the beginning and end of the year, and gift exchanges with their best friends at Christmas. Plan birthday parties, buy cheesy decorations, and learn the names of their friends' moms. Remember to coordinate playdates and swim lessons, and tell them they look beautiful every morning when they walk downstairs for school. Sing silly karaoke and plan living-room picnics on Friday nights.

If God calls me home, you will no longer just be the protector who holds their hands when crossing the street—you'll be the one who holds their hearts through bullies and breakups and the torturous days of adolescence and the stress of wedding planning.

I pray I can watch them become women and one day hold their babies in my arms. But if I can't, you need to carry them through. Remember what it was like raising them—the tantrums, the milestones, and the growing pains—so you can be the voice on the other end of the phone when desperate calls come about husbands, children, and life. Sweet husband, you need to continue to be their protector and biggest fan while also being their confidant, comforter, and emotional supporter.

And dear husband, if I am called home before we are old and gray, I need you to know I love you more than my own life, and I know you will raise our girls into women who love others as much as I loved you all.

Stacey Tadlock is the author of *Faithfully Failing*, where she encourages women through Scripture when they feel they are failing in faith, marriage, or motherhood.

Thank You, Mr. Pete

JILL ROBINSON

Heroes can be found in the most unlikely places.

Often our little ones idolize superheroes, athletes, or first responders. Some yearn to be astronauts. Many are enthralled at the idea of driving a large tractor, flying an airplane, or piloting a boat. They want to save lives as a doctor or a veterinarian. Some want to perform onstage or under the lights.

Not my youngest. His first hero was our neighborhood crossing guard, Mr. Pete.

Mr. Pete was a retired gentleman who waited at the corner each morning to help kids cross the street on their way to school. He would sit in his folding chair, waiting for the children to come by, then raise his stop sign to usher everyone safely across. My youngest saw him do this four times a day, but I never thought much of it.

One morning, after returning from dropping his older brother off at school, my then four-year-old was in the backyard playing while I cleaned up the morning breakfast disaster. I was keeping an eye on him through the window and saw him sitting quietly in one of our folding chairs. He had arranged two large orange safety cones on either side of him.

After a few minutes of sitting quietly, he stood up and lifted a tennis racket high above his head. He stood for a few moments before lowering the racket and returning to his chair. As I watched him repeat this over and over, it dawned on me that he was pretending to be Mr. Pete, complete with his chair, stop sign, and crosswalk. I was able to sneak a few photos before my camera-shy little one caught me. He repeated this make-believe ritual a few mornings a week.

That Christmas, we gave Mr. Pete one of these photos, along with a card and homemade cookies to thank him for keeping our kids safe. He, in turn, gave us a Chicago Cubs ornament for our Christmas tree, even though he was a White Sox fan.

In the years that followed, he watched my boys grow, and eventually my little crossing guard got to walk to school himself under Mr. Pete's watchful eye. We learned Mr. Pete used his chair due to heart problems; sometimes he would be gone for a few days, then come back when he was feeling better—until the day he didn't return. Our walk to school would never be the same. No more jokes about the current baseball rivalry. No more Christmas ornaments exchanged for homemade treats.

In the sympathy card we sent to his wife, I included the photo of that little boy pretending to be the kind man he saw helping us every morning. I wanted his family to know we would always think of Mr. Pete waiting for us at the corner. I wanted them to know what he meant to our family.

Mr. Pete didn't wear a cape. He didn't have superpowers. He wasn't paid millions, and he wasn't famous beyond our little part of the neighborhood. But it doesn't take great acts of bravery or special skills or heroic gestures to capture the heart of a child. All it takes is kindness and genuine interest to become the role model they need.

Each one of us has the potential to be a hero in our kids' lives. The mother who bandages a scrape, who sits by her child's bed when they're sick, who reads a bedtime story, or who braids hair is a hero in her child's mind. We don't need to do extraordinary things to be extraordinary.

Every Christmas when we place that Cubs ornament on our tree, we take a minute to remember both Mr. Pete and the small boys my kids used to be. We remember to be grateful for the common, everyday people in our lives. We remember what it means to be a role model.

And we say a silent, heartfelt "thank you" to Mr. Pete.

Jill Robinson has been published in *Chicken Soup for the Soul*, *Little Old Lady Comedy*, and *The Order of Us*. Follow her on Instagram (@firstdraftdotblog).

Words and Wings

ESTHER GOETZ

The faint aroma of yesterday's snuffed-out vanilla bean candle wafts through my office, the jar marked with sooty residue.

I stand and stare into what seems like an eternity gone by, my body still but unsettled, lost in thoughts that swirl around like a pinwheel on a breezy summer day.

Another vanilla bean candle jar sits on my desk, this one having been thoroughly emptied and cleaned. It has one little paper rectangle inside, with words carefully written on one side. Next to the jar is a pile of ninety-nine neatly folded squares, already read. They call out to me, sending me into a state of sadness woven tightly with joy.

Every morning for the past three months, I've looked forward to the message of love I would receive from my newly-flown-the-nest daughter. As a gift to her words-of-affirmation mom, she penned a few words on one hundred precisely cut pieces of colored paper and affixed a small butterfly sticker to the bottom right corner of each one.

Some speak of her favorite memories of just the two of us in the mayhem of a large family. One tells the long-forgotten story of the time I prayed for the referee who gave me a technical foul when I coached her sixth-grade basketball team. I had yelled (quite loudly) at this referee for putting one of my ponytailed girls in all kinds of danger (or so I vehemently felt in that competitive moment), and I had been commanded to sit down and not get up again. After-sports car rides are funny like that, allowing opportunity to pray for adversaries in the form of referees at children's playoff games.

Other notes express her favorite family traditions—ones I often feel I forced my kids to endure—like waiting until her dad got home from his long commute for us to have as many dinners as possible together as a family. It didn't matter if it was 8 p.m., the kids were starving, it was pizza, or the meal had to be sandwiched between all the after-school practices, activities, and homework. Family dinner was family dinner.

Most of them articulate unique reasons she loves me, her beautiful mess of a mom. One morning, I read this: *I love you because you don't shy away from hard conversations.* The words jumped out at me, catching me off guard. I sat down as tears tumbled down my cheeks. You see, this girl of mine is an "avoider," and I am a "chaser" during the conflicts we battle through—not a pretty sight. I pictured myself banging on her locked bedroom door saying, "Come out and talk about this (or else)!"

And the butterfly stickers? She knows me. She knows that in my worst and most anxious times, I believe God shows up for me in the form of butterflies. Sometimes on little-girl dresses. Or fluttering through the air and landing on my shoulder. On collages on the sides of buildings in Los Angeles. In memes on social media. Even in sticker form on the mammogram machine (true story). This girl knows me.

I snap back to consciousness, tenderly scooping out that final note, wanting to unwrap it and devour the words, yet not wanting to at the same time.

What will it be? A memory? A tradition? A love note? I secretly hope it will sum up all three in some beautiful crescendo.

Gathering myself, I pull it out, seeing the familiar writing and the winged creature in the corner.

The words aren't grand, but rather simple. They do their job.

I love you, Mom, because you are fully yourself with me.

What more can I ask for? What more can I hope for? What more can I want as a mom?

I spend the next hour rereading each note, every maternal emotion coursing through me once again, treasuring each thoughtful word that's been committed to paper by this daughter I love so dearly.

I'm not sure what to do now. Should I lock them safely away in a memory box for my grandchildren to read someday? Organize them by category and put them in a document on my computer in case there's a fire? (Only moms think about this stuff.) Leave them in the jar on my desk, taking one out the mornings I need to feel the love?

I may do all those things at some point. But for now, I'll just sit here with these precious papers scattered around me, light my vanilla bean candle, and allow the scent of pure love to envelop me once again.

Esther Goetz writes with a fierce passion to restore hope for the sacred space where hearts and homes meet.

A Mother
Never Really Dies

CHELSEA OHLEMILLER

✕

She watches as they place her mother in the ground. They say we're buried six feet under, but as she watches, it feels so much farther. With each inch the casket lowers, it's as if her mother is drifting miles and miles away, vanishing beneath soil as dark as this very moment.

The world now refers to her as "motherless," but this is a name and a title she doesn't accept. It does not describe her. Yes, she has a mother who died. But that truth doesn't change her beloved title of daughter, and it certainly doesn't erase the title of her mother. Nothing can take those things away, even if the world is determined to redefine them.

She stands there refusing to say goodbye, instead clinging to her belief in something greater. She stands firm in a powerful hope that this isn't the end of her mother's story. She doesn't tell this delicate truth to the others who watch. It's as if this is her last secret with her mother.

This will become the moment she knows her mother is in heaven—but she also feels her tethered to her heart and soul by an undeniable gravity. Death has changed her reality, but it has also created an understanding of the beautiful ways a mother's influence remains. Maybe that's a mother's biggest superpower—her ability to live on after her heart stops beating and her breath has been spent.

She wipes her tears and glances at the people beside her. They are family and friends and people she knows well, but in this moment, they are simply shadows, bystanders to her pain, to this fragile transformation of a mother's love. Things will be different now, and she knows it. Having someone you love in heaven changes things.

While others think this is the end, this daughter sees it differently. A mother's love and influence can never die, even after her last breath. And she knows mothers can never really die if they leave behind pieces of their hearts—and she is one of them.

She didn't become motherless when her mother went to heaven. She became a daughter with a mother here and there, in heaven and in her own heart. She became someone with a legacy to create and continue. Now she understands the strength of a mother. It's the kind of strength that can bear the weight of six feet of dirt, a name carved in stone, and the journey to eternity—and still show up for her child. That's the infinite life and love of a mother.

Chelsea Ohlemiller is a wife, mother, and advocate for the grief experience. She is best known for her blog, *Happiness, Hope & Harsh Realities*.

She Learned That from Her Mother

AMY JUETT

✕

Back and forth, back and forth. She rocked her baby girl on that late September day in 1960. She didn't believe rocking spoiled babies; she believed babies were born to be rocked. She must have learned that from her mother.

Her baby grew up and rocked her own baby girl—me—on that early April day in 1987. Mom lived just down the road from Grandma in the stucco house with blue kitchen cupboards. Hours were spent there rocking me back and forth as I grew from baby to toddler. Even into my childhood, when nightmares interrupted my sleep, Mom would sit in her rocker and rock me until my tears subsided and my eyes slow-blinked with the urge to sleep again. She knew a little rocking could fix a million different problems. She must have learned that from her mother.

I rocked my firstborn baby girl by the lights of the Christmas tree that early December night of 2011. Before then, I had no idea the depth of a mother's love. Though those early days proved neither as blissful nor as easy as I'd imagined, the hours rocking my sweet baby are ones I will cherish forever. My rocking chair became an oasis of rest in the unfamiliar desert of early motherhood.

Long after the newborn days, I rocked—through teething and sickness and sometimes just because. During morning snuggles and bedtime stories and plenty of moments in between, we rocked. Back and forth, back and forth.

Three boys came after that first baby girl, and I rocked them too. Back and forth, from midnight nursing sessions to midday naps, from sibling spats to bumps, bruises, and broken bones. That rhythmic motion brought a loving comfort to both the rocked and the rocker, whether the one I rocked was covered in dirt or fresh from the bath, sleepy or silly, healthy or sick, newborn, toddler, preschooler, or lanky child. I learned that from my mother.

I rocked that mid-April day in 2021. At her bedside, I held her hand as she grew closer to heaven's gate, while within my womb, my baby fluttered. Love had come full circle. Her daughters bent over her, gently wiping her cheek, brushing back her silvery hair, and singing favorite hymns of comfort. My children, her great-grandchildren, came in and out adjusting blankets, retrieving tissues, singing "Jesus Loves Me," and providing hugs and laughter at just the right moments. The generations of baby girls she had rocked and the men who loved them gathered to love and care for her, the one who had always loved and cared for them.

In these last hours, we wished we could simply pick her up and rock her as she had rocked us. You see, it wasn't just the joy of rocking babies she had taught us—it was the meaning of love. The love of a mother for her child, passed down from generation to generation. An unconditional love that garnered love in return in the ebb and flow of life.

I rocked my youngest baby today, the same one who fluttered in my womb by Grandma's bedside. My thoughts turn to Grandma often as I rock this child. If she were here now, her eyes would be alight with love and joy at the sight of a new great-grandbaby to be rocked. She would admonish me to make sure my baby girl was thoroughly burped, sufficiently rocked, and wearing a hat. I would reassure her I kept the baby out of drafty places, and she would remind me, "They grow so fast."

And, oh, don't I know it. I look at my firstborn baby, who isn't a baby anymore. Now when we rock, her legs stick off the edge of the chair, a reminder she won't fit on my lap much longer. She's almost ten—halfway to the age I married my husband. In the blink of an eye, it will be my baby sitting in the rocking chair rocking her own baby with all the love of a mother spilling from her heart. The hours she will spend rocking will become treasures she'll store forever in her memory.

She's learning that from her mother.

Amy Juett is a large-family homeschooling mom and writer who encourages and equips Christian mothers to thrive in their faith, motherhood, homemaking, and homeschooling.

Mothers Know
When to Round Up

KIT TOSELLO

When my son returned from his first year of college, he had changed in ways that made my mama heart swell with pride. Still, I kept looking beyond the chiseled jaw and the five o'clock shadow into his eyes, searching for a glimpse of the boy-child I remembered. My heart wanted to reconnect with him on a level he'd outgrown. And my head kept what-iffing. *What if this is my last chance to impart a few profound doses of mom wisdom?*

A sad thing happened when I gave in to those impulses. My son lost some of the emotional ground he'd gained while we were apart. And the vibe in our home grew weird.

This is where my own mom's wisdom saved me, and I've tried to channel it for the sake of all three of my adult kids: round up.

See, whenever summer waned and those big, yellow buses began trolling the neighborhood, rehearsing their routes, Mom took us kids on a pilgrimage to Kinney Shoes. The style was ours to choose, and from season to season I graduated from saddle shoes to Keds to clogs to Earth Shoes (can you dig it?) to Wallabees.

But when it came to size, Mom made the call. Never mind what number the clerk with the shiny foot-measuring device pronounced. My footwear had to last. So Mom rounded up, banking on what couldn't yet be seen—my growth.

And Mom rounded up in more significant ways. While I was still an awkward, unsure thirteen-year-old, she called me "responsible." I remember how that bene-diction felt like a pair of too-big flip-flops and how I sometimes tripped over myself trying to live up to it. I was one of the lucky ones whose parents believed in her—and said so.

Decades later, my mom, now eighty-four years old and a widow, experienced a sudden health decline, and it fell to me to look into assisted-living options. When I presented her with my research, expecting her to choose, can you guess what she said?

"I trust your judgment."

What? Most days, I can't even decide what to eat for lunch. This decision, this pair of shoes, was way beyond my size! Still, I couldn't do anything other than meet the challenge.

Our goal is to grow healthy and whole adults with a sense of agency over their choices. People who, when faced with hard things, will rise to the occasion. That means I need to get used to telling my kids, "I know you've got this, but I'm here if you need help." To affirm them when they're unsure—and to admit when I'm the unsure one. To celebrate the growth that's sure to come.

Saying "I believe in you" is a good start. But saying "I trust your judgment" when hard evidence to that effect is still forthcoming? That's graduate-level parenting. I'm bound to fall short at times. But I can do it.

After all, I'm still growing too.

Kit Tosello, an award-winning writer, is a wife, mom, and nana living in a small Oregon mountain town. Find her on Instagram and Facebook.

PART 9

SO GOD MADE A MOTHER

beautiful

×

**Sometimes a mother struggles
to recognize the woman in the mirror.
Her body is softer,** her eyes are tired, **and
lines crease her once smooth skin. Love
did that**—and though she might not
always see it, **it makes her more
beautiful every day.**

HER VIEW FROM HOME

The Sheets

LESLIE MEANS

X

I don't make my bed. I'm not one of those people who says, "If you wake up and make your bed, you will accomplish something right away and you're bound to have a productive day!"

No.

When I wake up, I head straight to the coffee pot, and that means I'll have a productive day.

But back to making my bed. I don't. Except for one occasion: when I have to wash the sheets. I don't like doing that either, but dirty sheets are disgusting, so I do.

I washed our sheets one winter morning. It had been a crazy day full of Christmas cookies and holiday events, and all I wanted to do was walk upstairs after a long Christmas movie and fall into bed.

But there was a problem: the sheets were still in a pile on our bed, waiting to be made. I asked Kyle if he would please put the sheets on our bed.

He laughed and said no.

I smirked and made some smart remark, then proceeded to drag my tired body into our bedroom to put those Christmas sheets on the bed.

But when I got to our room, it was already made. The fitted sheet was tucked, the comforter was placed, and the pillows were even fluffed.

My husband made the bed without telling me. And I wanted to cry happy, tired tears. I didn't have to make the bed! I didn't have to make the bed!

And that sums up nearly two decades of marriage.

Yes, we've been married for a while now, but when I was just twenty-three years old, walking down the aisle, butterflies flying, so anxious to marry that handsome, tall, kind, loving man, I didn't know then what I know now—that marriage is made up of a million little things.

The grand gestures are wonderful, of course, but with a mortgage, student loans, three babies, a cat, two jobs, volunteer gigs, and a partridge and a pear tree, the big things don't happen nearly as often as we'd like.

And that's okay. Because the little things are the glue that holds it all together. It's when he gets the kids ready for school each morning so I can take my time. It's the hot water for coffee and scraped windshields on icy days. It's coming to my rescue when my car breaks down or when I run out of gas (both literally and figuratively).

It's squeezing my hand when the contractions squeezed harder, and rocking those babies during middle-of-the-night shifts. It's walking by my side, sometimes hand in hand, sometimes behind, sometimes leading just so.

It's cleaning the kitchen and making dinner and singing songs with our girls. It's school projects and church functions and outings with friends. It's laughing with my family and never hesitating to help my parents with a project. It's honoring and protecting and cherishing my heart.

And it's making our bed, just because he knew that meant I wouldn't have to.

Kyle loves me so well because he knows my whole heart—the jagged edges and mushy middle and everything in between, and he thinks it's beautiful. It's the heart of a wife, a mother, a friend, a daughter, a dreamer—a lot like the one beating in your chest right now.

The heart of a mother is powered by love and grace and selflessness and faith. You'll see all those things reflected in these next several stories, and I hope they remind you just how beautiful you are.

My Metaphysical Pre-pregnancy Jeans

BRITTANY MENG

✕

I had a favorite pair of jeans in college—soft, with just the right amount of stretch—that hugged my curves in all the right places. I felt fabulous in those jeans: sexy, confident, and my best self. When we were twenty-one and dating in college, they always brought a cheeky grin to my husband's face.

After I had my twins at twenty-three, I clung to those jeans. I sighed heavily when they caught my eye as I put laundry away. Occasionally I pulled them out of the drawer and tried to squeeze into them, shimmying them up my hips, sucking in my gut, and holding my breath as I tried to button them.

But even when I lost the baby weight, they never fit again. Or, I should say, they never fit the same. My hips were wider, my booty was bigger, my stomach was softer. My body had changed completely.

I had changed completely.

Now, as a mother of five, I often reflect on how much I've changed. I'm proud of the mother I've become and the woman I challenge myself to be.

But now that my youngest baby, my only girl, is soaring through her toddler years and sprinting toward preschool, I've realized I haven't fully recovered since I had her. While I've physically and emotionally recovered from that difficult pregnancy and C-section, I feel like I haven't gotten my life back since she was born.

Caring for five children required me to let go of everything I built in my life outside of being a mother. Between living overseas during a difficult military assignment, pressing through a deployment, and enduring a pandemic, I had no choice but to let it all go so I could survive.

Sometimes I pause and look around at the life I've built for myself and wonder, *What happened to everything I worked so hard for?* I find myself reaching for castles in the sky, glorious structures I've fashioned out of thin air. When I try to pull them close in an attempt to cling to the past, they slip through my fingers.

And then I think again about those jeans—my favorite, fit-like-a-glove, sexy jeans—as I contemplate how long it's taken me to recover my life after my final baby, how nothing seems to fit, how I'm trying to find me again.

I think I've been trying to fit into a pair of metaphysical pre-pregnancy jeans, but they don't fit anymore. That part of my life is gone. It's changed. *I've* changed.

This realization has taken me by surprise because I've always been able to "bounce back" to my life and my goals after each baby. But the shift that took place after my daughter was born shook the foundation of my life.

I'm learning how to stand up again, how to use my legs and take tentative steps forward on new, untrodden paths. While my body has fully recuperated, my soul is still trying to recover. It's getting there. In the meantime, I'm learning to look at my life through new eyes.

The ache for what was squeezes tight sometimes, but I can't wear my old life anymore, just like I can't wear those college jeans comfortably after kids. There's grief in the letting go, in unclenching my fingers from a season well lived, from goals and achievements accomplished, from work and vocations that served their time and purpose. I eventually found new jeans, ones that were comfortable and made me feel confident, ones that made my husband raise his eyebrows and pull me into the laundry room for the type of kiss that promises more after the kids go to bed.

As my last baby grows into a little girl, I have faith that I'm still growing too. There is joy ahead, fresh work and dreams, renewed confidence, different ways of being alive. I'm moving through all the changes and finding new ways of becoming myself.

Brittany Meng is a mom of four boys and one girl. She hosts *The Motherhood Metamorphosis* podcast and writes at *The Bam Blog.*

I Will Always Remember Your Baby

JENNIFER ROSS

×

It was a Friday afternoon. I'd been called in to help, which usually meant we were in the middle of a baby boom at the hospital, yet it was strangely quiet when I walked into the nursery.

My job that evening was to do something I'd never done before: serve as the bereavement nurse for your baby.

Your sweet baby was swaddled and lying in a bassinet in a private room in the back. Your little one looked like all the other infants—same blanket with requisite stripes, same soft-knit hat with light blue and pink threads woven into the pattern, same bassinet. But there were a few things missing. There was no crib card with the vital statistics, no supplies in the drawers for future diaper changes. And your baby was quiet, too quiet.

He never took that precious first breath.

You had no way of knowing his lungs had never developed. You had no way of knowing as he kicked and rolled around in your belly that those movements would cease when he was born. It was all a shock.

You never held him. You said if you did, you would never let go. This was not how it was supposed to happen. This was not the way you imagined it.

I was your baby's nurse, and I want you to know I never forgot him—or you.

I bathed your precious boy just as I would any other newborn, but with extra tenderness. I washed his auburn hair and combed it. I snugly fastened his first and only diaper. Before I dressed him in his special white outfit, complete with a hat, another nurse and I took photos of his hands and feet. We put him on his stomach, with his legs underneath him and his diapered baby bottom in the air. For a moment as we snapped photos of him, we smiled at his cuteness and momentarily forgot our sadness.

I cradled him in the crook of my arm for a photo, being careful not to include my face. I just wanted to show him being loved. I snipped a bit of his hair and carefully put it in a clear bag with a blue ribbon. With my best handwriting, I filled out his hospital birth certificate, including his tiny footprints.

I gathered all we had of your little boy and placed it in a memory box. I'd shot a whole roll of film. Those would be developed and placed with the negatives in the keepsake box. I glanced over the mementos. Was it enough?

Reluctantly I undressed your sweet boy and placed the clothes, his blanket, his hat, and even his diaper in the box.

I spent some time alone with your baby. I talked to him and prayed over him. I hope that was okay.

The best part of my job has always been watching a baby take their first breath. The worst part is knowing certain babies never do that, despite our best efforts, and a family is changed forever.

When I left that night, it was a sweet spring evening with all the promise of fresh growth. The dichotomy between the sadness in my heart and the joy of a new season did not escape me.

You left the hospital the next day and refused the memory box. It was all too much.

I thought of you often and wondered how you were doing. Several months passed, and soon it was the first week of May, with flowers bursting into full bloom, offering hints of Mother's Day. Work was steady with many births. I answered the phone one afternoon, expecting it to be one of the new moms or dads or maybe a pediatrician. Instead, it was you.

I didn't know it at first, but I recognized you as soon as you said, "I had a baby at your hospital a few months ago . . ." Then your voice caught as you said, "He died, and I heard you have a copy of his footprints."

It was no accident I answered your call.

"I remember your sweet boy, and I'm so glad you called," I replied. "We do have his footprints, along with some other mementos. You can come get them anytime."

You sniffled and said you'd be right over. I hung up, hoping the items in the box would bring comfort to your hurting heart.

My plan was to give you the box myself. I let the charge nurse know you were coming in, but when you arrived, I was busy helping with a delivery and you left before we had a chance to connect.

Your son would be in his twenties now, had he lived. I hope life has treated you well. I hope you made some sort of peace with what happened. You will never get over it . . . that just isn't possible. But I hope you know I never forgot your sweet boy, or you. His life was brief, but he touched my heart that day—and together we hold him in our hearts forever.

Jennifer Ross writes her blog, *See Jenn Tri,* on her typewriter, annoying her family and her dog—who still love her and her writing.

The Truth
about Your Body

NATASHA CARLOW

×

I have been overweight my entire life, and no one is more aware of what that means than I am. I've heard every side of it. Doctors who ignore me or identify my weight as the cause of every illness. Friends who use me as a size comparison. Family members who point out every change in my weight. Sales clerks who insist the top will fit when I can already see it's too small. Strangers who think I take up too much space or, even worse, think my body type implies I'm an easy target for sexual conquests. Yes, I am fully aware of what it all means. And I am aware my body and my health are important and are my responsibility.

I am also a woman and a mother who wants to spare her daughter and son from judging themselves and their bodies based on the opinions of others. My daughter often notes things about my body and asks me if her body will look the same—will her face look like mine, or will she have to use this product or that? Answering these questions has shown me I still have a long way to go, and perhaps that's one of the reasons God made me a mother.

Many things are true about my daughter. She can be happy and silly one minute, then quiet and pensive the next. She can be brave at times, and so shy at other times she needs to bury her face in my side. To me, she is the most beautiful being who ever lived. It isn't just that she is beautiful—it's that she sees beauty in everything. A baby on television will make her gasp with joy. An injured puppy on the side of the road will bring tears to her eyes. Her brother's accomplishments will elicit a celebratory dance, because his wins are her wins and all wins must be acknowledged. Her prayers are filled with the needs of others. She is concerned about the state of the world around her and is secure in her love for and faith in God. She is active and conscientious about her health.

So I want her to know what's true about her body, which is why we will continue to have conversations about it. Her young one will change and mature as my older one ages. Some talks will happen in private; others will be out in the open. Some will leave us in stitches; others will be whispered and tinged with pain. But we won't shy away from them.

These are the things I want my daughter to remember about her body:

Your body honors God. This body God gave you should be used to bring honor to Him each day, both in what you do with it and how you treat it. Discipline and self-control can help you honor God and show gratitude for your body.

Your body will be judged—love it anyway. I dread the day someone calls you fat. To think a stranger could hold any power over your self-image makes me hurt. But you must learn to love your body now, not for the way it looks but for the opportunities it affords you. You can see, hear, smell, taste, and touch. You can think and love and run and jump and play. None of this is affected by anyone's opinions. So please, please love your body.

Your body works hard for you—cherish it. I have no preconceived notions of what you should look like. All bodies are beautiful and valid, so cherish the one you have. My own body gave me my children, and for that I will be forever grateful. Whatever you desire for your life—career, goals, relationships, motherhood—it all begins with a body that works hard.

Your body is only a part of who you are. As important as your body is, remember it's only one part of you. You are so much more than your physical self. A healthy body is important, but so is emotional health, mental health, and spiritual well-being. These are the things that matter most.

Your body is transient—live for a higher purpose. This lesson is perhaps most difficult of all: I want you to remember that bodies die. Death is a hard but inevitable truth of living. One day the ones you love will die, and you will too. What happens next is far better than anything that will happen here on earth. Live for the greater promise of the life that's to come, where there will be no broken bodies or illness or pain—only joy unlike anything we've ever known.

You are more than a number on a scale. You are more than a size. You are more than any label someone might slap on you. You are valuable because you are uniquely you—precious and beautiful and made in the image of God.

Natasha Carlow is a wife and a mother of two. She is the author of *Happy Tears and Rainbow Babies* and *Mike Nero and the Superhero School.*

Twenty-Two Inches
of Femininity

NANCY BRIER

✕

"You can always change your mind at the last minute if it doesn't feel right," my husband said.

He was trying to get me to meet a man he'd met on the Internet, and I wasn't comfortable with it. Gary's always been adventurous, but lately he'd been spending a lot of time on the computer and had gone down an online rabbit hole. Before I knew it, he'd found somebody named Jon who lived in Minnesota, and the two of them were talking and exchanging personal information.

"Will you at least talk to him?" Gary asked. "Then if you still don't want to do it, I'll drop the idea."

He dialed and handed me the phone. Jon answered.

I exhaled slowly and introduced myself.

After a few minutes, I had to admit he sounded nice. I asked him a lot of questions, and he answered all of them, taking his time and encouraging me to talk too. Finally, after major hesitation, I booked a trip.

"Who goes to Minneapolis in January?" my friend asked over coffee on the appointed day when I whispered my plans. "Especially when you live in California?"

Later that morning, I dug long underwear out of storage, along with a thick hat and my only winter coat. I pulled my gray wheelie bag down from the shelf and started to pack. *What am I doing?*

Then I headed to the bank, withdrew cash, and tucked the bills into the zippered compartment of my purse. I didn't want a paper trail reminding me of my foolishness—my vanity, even—if the whole thing went wrong. *What if I regret what I'm about to do?*

Gary and our daughter drove me to the airport. On the way, I checked and rechecked my paperwork, hotel reservations, and money. I hugged my family goodbye, boarded the plane, and planned to meet Jon the next day.

It was negative six degrees in Minneapolis, and piles of snow and dirty ice were mounded along the roadways. After twenty years of marriage, I felt odd about being in this unfamiliar city alone, with plans to meet a man who would change me.

The next morning, I plugged Jon's address into my phone, bundled into my coat, and shoved my hat down as far as it would go. I walked on icy sidewalks, examining addresses carefully, looking for numbers that matched my notes. I still couldn't believe I was doing this.

Finally I pulled open a glass door, and a surge of warmth shocked my frozen cheeks. Christian rock blared from a speaker. In the empty shop, I sank into a leather chair, staring at myself in the mirror. Neat rows of product made symmetrical designs along the walls. Unlike Gary, Jon turned out to be tall and dark and outgoing. He told me he keeps a running conversation with God, and sometimes he laughs at jokes only he and God are privy to.

While he talked, he opened a cabinet, pulled out a cape, and draped it around my shoulders. Then he rolled a table near my chair, wheels creaking over linoleum.

Tentatively, I took off my hat.

Jon rubbed his hands over my cancer-ravaged, inch-long, baby-soft new hair. "We can do it," he said with a smile. "It's long enough."

Someone else's hair was piled on the table along with a hot glue gun. With practiced hands, Jon took strands of hair, dabbed one end in glue, and attached the bundle to a wisp of my own hair. I watched while my chemo head disappeared under a canopy of blonde. Nodules of glue butted against my scalp, each one a pebble the size of a pea, each attached to glorious, wavy hair.

"You girls come from all over the world now," Jon said, pointing to a before-and-after photo. "But she was my first chemo girl. I'll never forget her."

My guilt for this indulgence started to abate, and I settled in.

Seven hours later, a new me emerged. It wasn't chemo me. It wasn't cancer me. It was just me.

Jon guided me to a sink, and the exotic fragrance of Moroccan oil filled my senses—my first shampoo in nearly a year. Breathing in, I felt like a woman. A normal woman at a hair salon. Then he combed out my new hair, twenty-two inches of beautiful femininity.

When Jon spun my chair around and I saw myself in the mirror, my cancer was gone. Flushed with satisfaction, and even giddy, I handed Jon the cash from my purse. "Take the hat too," I said.

Outside Jon's shop door, the frigid Minneapolis air felt fresh and invigorating on my skin. Waving goodbye, I made my way back home to embrace my roles. I hadn't stopped being a woman, a wife, a mother. But now I felt like her again.

Nancy Brier is regrowing her hair with her balding husband and their teenage daughter, whose hair is perfect.

Dear Daughter, Love Keeps Going

CASSIE GOTTULA SHAW

✕

Overwhelmed by a heap of cardboard boxes, I knelt on the dusty concrete floor and searched for one with my name on it. When I spotted it at the bottom of the pile, I slid the others out of the way until I could sit on the floor, with my legs tucked underneath me.

The box was closed in the standard over-under tuck I'd once heard called a bookman's fold, the edges worn away by time and the black print faded. It had been sitting in that garage for a long time. But now my parents were leaving the home I'd grown up in—the home I'd always returned to—and it was time to collect my things.

So many memories were stored in that box, it felt like I was stepping right into the past. Its contents weren't grand or exciting, at least not to anyone but me: yellowing newspapers, a stack of photos, a few beloved paperbacks, and countless ideas and doodles scribbled in a bundle of notebooks. And a tiny bag at the bottom of the box I nearly missed altogether. My heart dropped into my stomach as buried memories resurfaced. I opened the bag and emptied its contents into my hands.

The two women's rings were exactly as I remembered them. Both set in white gold bands, the first was a simple solitaire, a tiny marquise-cut diamond from the first time I fell in love, and the second was a three-diamond melee with a mother of pearl inlay, given to me a handful of years later.

At pivotal points in my life, each ring represented love to me. Each was a promise. But those relationships weren't meant to last a lifetime, and over the years they crumbled. As they fell apart, they released my heart, which dropped to the ground and shattered. Such is often the tale of young love.

I decided to keep the rings.

Over time my heart healed, and there was no more pain inside the memories. Those rings became a symbol of how I'd grown and who I'd become. They were a representative of self-love, of moving forward. That was something I imagined passing along to my children someday. So long before she was born, I decided to save the rings as a lesson for my future daughter. I slipped them into a little bag and hid them away for more than a decade.

She's a preschooler now, my little girl, full of joy and wonder. She loves big and unconditionally and without expectation. I don't want to imagine her first heartbreak, but inevitably it will come. When it does, I'll share something special with her—an intimate piece of myself and my story, with a reminder that will sparkle on her finger or hang around her neck or rest atop her nightstand.

I know a little something about it, I'll tell her. I know about falling in love and splitting apart. I know about the weight of broken promises. I've been there, in that place where the hurt is so deep you think you can't go on. Sometimes it feels like another lifetime, but other times it feels like yesterday. I'll share with her what I went through, and I pray she'll share with me too.

I'll ask her to hold the rings in her hand. To study them. To think about who her mom was when she wore them. I'll tell her what they symbolize for me and what I hope she'll remember when she's hurting.

- You are never, ever alone. You can always go to your mama.
- Let yourself heal. It takes time. It takes tears. Let yourself experience your feelings.
- Remember that most things—even beautiful things—aren't meant to last. To everything there is a season. God has more in store for you.

- Don't look for a "good enough" kind of love. Don't look for a "they're doing their best" kind of love. Look for someone who will choose to love you the way you need and deserve to be loved—every day, for always.
- Heartbreak doesn't diminish your capacity for love. On the contrary, it readies you for something even deeper as it heals.
- This is only a part of your story. It feels monumental today, I know. But one day, even if you can't see it now, it will feel minuscule. So many things are going to happen to you. Big things, little things, hard things, incredible things, unimaginable things. Let them happen—let life happen.
- You will find your forever. I did. Imagine how different life would have been if I'd accepted forever any sooner.
- And I want you to understand—love will always keep going.

When love runs its course between two people, that love doesn't end—it multiplies. It splits into countless pieces, each one containing a bit of that love. You'll take those pieces with you: your renewed sense of compassion and your effort to be more understanding. The lessons you'll know for next time. The forgiveness that could rekindle old friendships. The self-love I hope you'll discover. And each piece is reflective of the Love that started it all. It creates a kaleidoscope of beauty out of the messy, the painful, and the hard.

Love keeps going. That means every moment is worth it.

Love won't fail you. It will always find you again.

But daughter, whenever you doubt, whenever you wonder, whenever your heart is hurting, look no further than your mama, who loves you more than anything. Forever.

Cassie Gottula Shaw explores themes of motherhood, mental health, self-discovery, and compassionate theology. She writes at *Girl, I've Got You* and *The Lovely Soul Disciples*.

I Wear My Heart
on My Sleeve

CAROLE JOHNSTON

✕

I take a deep, shaky breath to calm my nerves as the scent of bleach and antiseptic burns my nostrils. I'm lying on my back on a cushioned table, my left arm stretched out at an angle, the inside turned upward. I roll my head to the left to watch Christie, a woman with wide brown eyes and blonde hair cascading just past her shoulders, preparing her equipment with gloved hands. I've done this before, so I really shouldn't be nervous.

But this tattoo is going to be much bigger and much more important to me—because it's about my children.

When Christie finishes setting up her tools, she turns to me and winks. "Are you ready?" A loaded question. It had taken me a long time to get here.

I take another deep breath. "Yes."

Her expression takes a serious turn, and the tattoo machine starts to buzz. The anticipation in the air is electric. She leans over my arm, and I feel the needle pierce my skin. I train my eyes on the ceiling above and count the white tiles.

I can tolerate most of the pain, but there are a few moments it becomes too much. Before I can say anything, Christie seems to read my mind; she lifts the needle and wipes my arm with a damp paper towel, giving me a moment to catch my breath.

For years, I've wanted to get a tattoo of my children's names. I'd scroll through images online and save the ones I liked most. I'd get excited about them but could never commit to a design. Then months would go by before I thought about it again.

Until a friend's mom passed away unexpectedly.

That jolted me out of my complacency, and I suddenly felt an urgent need to stop stalling and get on with it. I began to look in earnest for a tattoo design.

A couple of weeks later, I stepped into a local tattoo parlor, with a printout of my favorite design clutched in my trembling hand. This was it. I was actually doing it.

An ocean of emotions flooded my body. Fear. Exhilaration. Hope. Determination.

I took an instant liking to Christie, with her piercings and inked arms. She was calm, soft spoken, and attentive. As we chatted, she studied my tattoo example and offered suggestions.

After careful consideration, I decided to get the tattoo on the inside of my left forearm. This was the exact spot my babies' heads, with their wispy blond hair, rested for hours—day and night—while I held them, fed them, and rocked them. I would try to memorize their faces, with their tiny, perfectly formed noses and lips, while they ate and slept. I tried to treasure every eyelash flutter, every murmur, every facial expression. When they were sleeping, I would lean down and sniff their sweet baby scent.

My right hand was often busy, holding a baby bottle, brushing back hair from their foreheads, adjusting their blanket. But my left arm had one job: to support my babies' precious heads, keeping them safe.

This is exactly where I wanted my tattoo. My left arm no longer has the job of cradling my babies. Now its job is to be a beautiful, daily reminder of my love for my children.

Christie and I came up with the perfect design. A delicate, curling black vine, representing me as their mama, runs down the center of my forearm. On one side, my daughter's name, Julia, is written in black cursive. On the other side, in matching font and color, is my son's name, Andrew. Near each name is a softly shaded purple flower, attached to the vine. These flowers represent each of my children, born of me, the vine. They also show my children's growth and beauty. I chose purple because it is a blend of pink and blue, my daughter and my son.

When I look at those two flowers, I think about precious moments with Andrew and Julia. The quiet feedings in the early morning light, just the two of us, before the world woke up. The sticky, pudgy hands holding my face still to plant a sloppy wet kiss there. The small arms eagerly reaching up to me when they wanted to be held.

To the left of Andrew's flower, near Julia's name, is a purple butterfly in flight. This image represents my two babies lost to miscarriage—the ones I didn't get to hold. The ones whose sweet heads never rested safely on my left arm. The ones who left too soon and flew to heaven while I lay below curled up in bed, with balled-up wet tissues strewn across my blankets.

As much as it pains me to look at this butterfly, I love it, because it represents my two babies who are safe in heaven and who now also rest safely on my arm, close to their earthly siblings forever.

When I think about Andrew and Julia growing up—and in some ways, growing away from me—my mama heart aches. When I think about my lost babies, gone too soon, my mama heart aches. When I think about the wait until my family of six will be together in heaven, my mama heart aches.

But every day, I see this beautiful tattoo of my children. Every day, I see my tender heart outside my body, permanently etched in ink on my skin. Every day, I see joy and pain, and I feel it all so deeply.

Because I wear my heart on my sleeve.

Carole Johnston lives in Canada with her husband, their two teenagers, and a very good dog. Follow her on Facebook and Instagram (@FamilyFunandDysfunction).

Strong in
These Boots

STEVIE SWIFT

✕

I have a pair of sand-colored Danner boots. I wore them as part of my Army uniform, with green socks pulled over my calves, my pant legs shoved into the boot tops, and my laces tucked carefully inside.

I walked through hard things in these boots. I carried heavy things in these boots. I survived painful things in these boots.

I thought I was weak, but in these boots, I learned I could shoulder what threatened to crush me.

I learned I could walk right up to that line where I wanted to quit, where every cell in my body screamed at me to give up. I could walk right up to it and step over it and keep walking.

In these boots, I learned I was strong.

And after the boots were no longer a requirement, after I'd retired the green socks and the uniform and the tucked-in laces, I still wore them.

On days when I wanted to quit, days I thought I didn't have anything left to give, I found strength when I put on my boots.

The day I took the LSAT, I almost stayed home. I'd scheduled the test months before, when I didn't know I'd be a newly single mom on test day. I didn't know I'd be looking for apartments. I didn't know I'd be looking for a car. I didn't know my son would hit his head minutes before it was time for me to leave.

So with my baby bleeding and crying, with my stomach in knots over the chaos of my life, the thought of leaving the house made me feel sick. I didn't want to get into a borrowed car, and I didn't want to sit for an hours-long test. I almost stayed home, but I didn't. I put on my boots and took the test, and I got the score and I went to law school.

In my boots, I felt strong.

When day-to-day responsibilities felt too heavy, when the groceries and the middle-of-the-night feedings and the daycare drop-offs and the fevers all felt too hard—I'd spend a day in my boots.

When I tapped my pencil against a list of bills and felt the crushing weight on my shoulders alone, I tapped the toe of my boots and remembered my shoulders are strong.

On mornings when getting up felt impossible, when I lay on my bed and stared at my infant son, wondering how I was going to do this on my own, I got up and I put on these boots. I slipped my feet inside and tightened the laces and thought about all the days I'd walked through in them. Somehow the day that had seemed impossible while I was in bed felt doable in the boots.

I wore them until they were garbage, until the soles started to break and I left pieces of boot everywhere I walked. Even then, I couldn't throw them out right away.

It wasn't the boots that made me stronger, I know. The boots just reminded me I've been strong before, I've had tough days before, I've done hard things before. Even without them, I'll keep walking farther than I thought I could, carrying more than I thought possible.

Even though I said goodbye to the boots, I'm not done with hard things. I'm not done pushing myself. I'm not done squeezing everything I can from this life.

As I finally lowered them into the garbage, I reminded myself of this again: it wasn't the boots that made me strong.

But I kept the laces, just in case.

Stevie Swift lives free, following Jesus, traveling, being Mom to The B, and writing poems about cheese.

Motherhood Chose Me

MARISA DONNELLY

✕

I always imagined motherhood as white linen sheets and a crib at the foot of my bed. A hand on my smooth, swollen belly. A flushed face and pistachio ice cream right out of the carton, talking about baby names with my husband as we matched each other, spoonful for spoonful.

I pictured a baby shower with a smile that couldn't be wiped from my face, fingertips running over the fabric of my dress, feeling for movement and subtle kicks. I imagined my parents, my sister, my best friend—all the people I loved just as excited as I was for this big moment. I envisioned bringing a child of my own flesh, blood, and heart into the world.

When I thought about motherhood, I pictured ultrasounds and appointments, nervous butterflies as the doctor searched for a heartbeat and my husband squeezed my hand. I thought about the quiet moments I would spend, reflecting on how it would feel to become entirely new, to shed the independence of being my own as I gained something that would be a part of me *forever*.

But becoming a mother was none of those things for me.

Becoming a mother was my stomach flip-flopping as I walked through the entrance of a small-town pumpkin patch and saw a young boy holding hands with the man I loved. It was an eight-year-old's hazel-brown eyes looking at me in wonder while the noise of carnival games, screaming kids, and petting zoo animals fell silent around me.

Becoming a mother was the moment this boy turned and handed me the prize he won from throwing darts. "Here . . . this is for you."

It was slowing my pace and stepping back to watch the two of them walk toward the inflatable slide and realizing this small, seemingly insignificant moment would be one I would never forget.

Becoming a mother was glasses and size five shoes. It was graphic novels and video games, snack wrappers and dirty fingers. It was handmade lunches and kisses on the forehead, and my heart swelling as I watched this little boy run off to the school playground and disappear in the crowd of other messy-haired kids.

Becoming a mother was the first "I love you" whispered in a dark bedroom as an echo to my lullaby. It was signing a lease and realizing this home was more than just a physical place; it was the space where love would knit us together as a family.

Becoming a mother was the first time my voice caught in my throat when I said "my son" and realized I meant it.

I always imagined motherhood to be an enormous, far-in-the-distance decision. I thought, like the forward thinker I am, that I would have time to be ready, to prepare. That I would know what I was doing and feel less afraid.

I thought I would choose my motherhood; it didn't cross my mind that my motherhood would choose me.

Becoming a mother was, in many ways, unexpected. It was saying yes to a man I loved and realizing I was saying yes to a little boy, too. It was understanding that love, for me, was more than just agreeing to be with someone. It was committing and knowing, beyond a doubt, I was here to stay.

For me, motherhood was the gravity of a single decision that would change the trajectory of my entire life. And yet it was a subconscious choice—one God undoubtedly designed for me long before I knew my own story.

The version of motherhood that chose me is different from what I expected. It's heavier—not in the sense of a burden, but in the sense that what I carry is an even more precious load. That's because it does not, and will never, fully belong to me.

But even though I didn't bring this boy into the world, he is still mine. I am no longer just me, no longer a single soul. I am attached to this boy and this man. There is an invisible thread—one not sewn by me, but one I acquired and wrapped around my heart—that has redefined who I am.

For me, motherhood is a patchwork quilt of people I chose. No, it's not the swollen belly. It's not the spoonful after spoonful of ice cream at midnight. It's not the flutter of a heartbeat on an ultrasound screen.

This motherhood is my phone number scrawled across a baseball glove, the ear-to-ear smile at school pickup, the "Please, just one more song" at bedtime. This motherhood is sneaking notes into lunchboxes, scouring grocery store aisles for snacks, imagining years down the road and planning our story.

This motherhood is different, yes, but this motherhood is beautiful. I choose this motherhood. And this motherhood chose me.

Marisa Donnelly, MEd, is a writer, editor, educator, small business owner (x2), host of *The VulnerABILITY Podcast*, and proud bonus mama of a teenager.

Stretch Marks

REBECCA NEVIUS

My feet hit the cobbled stone in slow, deliberate strides. On either side, small Cornish shops held treasures from the sea: kitschy mugs and hand-painted images of St. Michael's Mount, a medieval castle looking like a page out of Walt Disney's sketchbook. I couldn't believe this was our new home.

A few months earlier, my husband, Joel, and I had moved from our tiny apartment in California, packed all our belongings into a giant box, and headed to England.

The look on Joel's face as he unloaded my nine-foot longboard onto the London train platform still makes me smile. A little eye roll mixed with excitement: "Miles and miles of coastline, and you won't even be able to use it," he said, eyeing my growing belly.

I knew I was pregnant the night we cleaned out our apartment in Fullerton, California. My body knew it, and my heart felt it. Even though we hadn't met, that little human had already changed my life. I was a mom.

Joel and I joked about the wisdom of surfing while pregnant and agreed it was an option as long as I was careful.

Unfortunately, the board gathered dust the whole next month. It sat unused in our garage as I felt the pain of my first contraction. It flashed a purple blue as the ambulance pulled into our driveway, whisking me to the hospital an hour away in Treliske.

We took the tiny body down to the coast and buried it, my husband and I sitting hand over hand, our grief colliding with disbelief. And it hit me: nobody even knew I was a mother. I wanted stretch marks on my body so I would have something to show for my motherhood, but my arms were empty. I was a walking casket.

The following weeks were bitter. I was angry at myself, angry at God, and angry at Joel for no reason at all. Quaint little houses were old and dusty. Cute baby strawberries growing wild outside our front door were covered in slugs. *Figures,* I'd think, slamming the door to eat my whipped cream in peace. The seagulls annoyed me with their incessant cawing and swarming. *Why won't they just shut up?* Bike rides along the coast were just a reminder of where we'd left her. A reminder I wasn't really a mom anymore.

The thing about bitterness is it's really good at filling empty arms and replacing what you've lost with toxic grief, the kind of grief that never heals but lets you hold on longer to what you've lost. *How else will you hold on to your motherhood?* it whispered to me. *If you're happy, that means you didn't really love her.* And it was so much easier to fill my arms with lies than to actually walk through the pain.

Honestly, I was afraid. Dealing with the loss would mean healing, and didn't healing mean losing the only shred of motherhood I had left?

I was becoming numb even to the emotions I wanted to feel. Grief wasn't allowing me to hold on to my brief brush with motherhood—it was taking my heart, piece by piece.

Two months later, I found myself wandering through town along the historical route where pirates had pillaged and free traders had smuggled untaxed whiskey through underground tunnels. Walking had always been my way of relaxing, a place of silence, a way to let go. I knew something was wrong inside me. I knew if I didn't deal with it, I was threatening a full soul explosion down the road.

And then I came to it, a literal fork in the road. One side led up through town away from the coast; the other led down past the seawall, and eventually to the sea itself.

Bitterness had written its name on the uphill road, and it became clear to me that continuing on the angry road away from my pain was merely taking away what I wanted most: a mother's heart. Healing was written on the road to the sea, even though walking it would require me to feel deeper pain than I'd ever thought possible. I'd have to release my unborn baby, not just bury her. I'd have to choose joy and accept healing for my broken heart.

I never did get on the longboard that year.

I did eventually get to hold several babies in my arms. Cora is our youngest. She loves to nuzzle her head into my tummy, and this morning asked about that special skin on my belly as she pointed to my stretch marks. I told her she gave me those when she grew inside me, my body so big it almost burst. She asked if all mommies had stretch marks. I told her a lot of mommies do, but not all.

Some mothers have stretch marks in different places, the evidence of their motherhood not on their bodies or even in their arms. Their stretch marks are on the inside.

I learned I was a mom from that first pregnancy test so many years ago, but I didn't learn how to be a mother until my heart was broken.

Every Valentine's Day I think of her, the one by the sea, and the extraordinary gift she gave me. She taught me letting go is an essential part of being a mother. It's what helps us trust in a very big God. It's what allows our hearts to heal and mends us when all we want to do is rage and berate. It's choosing joy when that doesn't seem possible. It's what I'll do when they leave the house one day, all grown up, and I'm again left with empty arms.

This is the heart of every mother, whether she holds a child in her arms or not. She loves through the pain, not despite it. She bears stretch marks on her heart.

Rebecca Nevius, a mom with an MA in philosophy, is a writer and an illustrator, and the author of *God Is Bigger Than a Juice Box*, among others.

PART 10

SO GOD MADE A MOTHER

just like you

✕

"When you become a mother, there's no picking what to feel. You feel it all."

MAYA VORDERSTRASSE

The Best Part

✕

There's a china hutch that sits in the entryway of my home. I love its 1960s-meets-modern-day style. The hutch is dark brown and has four peg legs, a glass front, and small cabinets at the bottom.

I told Mom it's a style people today would love.

She nodded her head and said something like, "Whatever you say, Les," which is basically code for, "My daughter makes things up, but I do love her."

Although the look does fit my taste, there's also something about this piece that makes it a one-of-a-kind find.

It was Mom and Dad's.

This china hutch stood in the heart of my childhood home. Four framed senior photos sat on top, one for each of their girls—my sisters and me (I'm the baby of the family).

Inside, the hutch held family heirlooms: glass bowls, a china platter, plates from my grandmother. In the middle was a candy bowl filled with mints and, if we were lucky, small chocolates. That was always the best part.

The bottom drawers held photos from years past, which left the side drawers for a few holiday decorations—a turkey salt-and-pepper shaker and a Christmas serving dish, among other things. On occasion, when Mom's youngest was feeling lazy (yes, that's me), the drawers also held things like ornaments or small trinkets that didn't quite make it to the storage room.

Of all the items in my farmhouse, it was my favorite.

When Mom and Dad built their new home down the gravel road from our childhood home (where my sister and her husband live now), they left the china hutch behind. "It's just too bulky," they said. "We don't have room for it."

Immediately, I said I would take it.

It's been in my entryway for a few years now. On top sits a family photo and a covered wagon my oldest made in school. Inside, it holds china we received for our wedding, glass bowls, and plates from my grandmother. The bottom drawers are full of photos and important papers. I still get lazy and fail to put things in storage, so the side drawers tend to hold holiday trinkets and seasonal décor. And in the middle, there is, of course, a candy bowl filled with mints and chocolates. My kids think that's the best part. I do too.

"Les, did I ever tell you the story about that china hutch?" Mom asked me one day.

I'm always up for a good story. Especially if my mother, who tends to keep her life stories very private, is offering to share.

"When your dad was drafted to Vietnam, your sister and I lived with my mom and dad," she told me. "I was a secretary. I worked during the day, and Mom watched your sister." (My oldest sister, Lora, was only a month old when Dad was drafted. Dad was nineteen; Mom was eighteen.)

"When I earned my first paycheck, your grandma told me to buy something with it. I thought that sounded like a great idea. I bought a dishwasher and that china hutch with my very first one."

And just like that, Mom's china hutch went from one of my favorite items in my home to my very favorite.

It tells a story—of a hardworking mother who loved her family well. A woman who worked hard all her life—first as a secretary, then as a stay-at-home-mom, and always helping my dad on the farm. When the farming crisis of the eighties hit, she worked outside the home again, this time as a registered nurse. She's retired now, but her work ethic lives on.

Can a simple old piece of furniture really tell a story? It does for me. And it's one I'm proud to be part of. Maybe my kids will have their own version someday too.

Every one of us has a story to tell. It might be like my mom's—about hard work and family and steadfast love. It might be filled with heartbreak. It could be a story you're just beginning to write, unsure of the direction it will go. You know what we all have in common, though?

The world needs your story. Even if it feels like it's not fancy enough or it's just not that interesting. I promise you—it matters, because you matter. To your kids. To your spouse. To God.

So I want you to promise me something. Tell it. Tell it in the way you show up, every day. Tell it in the way you tuck the blankets just so around your sleeping babies (no matter how old they are). Tell it in the way you love as only you can, and know it's a masterpiece. Because *you* are a masterpiece.

When God made a mother, He had you in mind—imperfect, incredible, irreplaceable you.

And I, for one, think that's definitely the best part.

No One Else but You

MAYA VORDERSTRASSE

When you think about a woman before kids, you think about all the sleep she used to get and the events she got to attend. You think about the hobbies she used to have and the freedom she enjoyed.

When you think about a woman after kids, you think about responsibilities, schedules, and chores. You think about restless nights and rushed showers.

But then you become a mother—and all your perceptions are mashed together into your new life. When you become a mother, there's no picking what to feel. You feel it all.

You start by feeling surprised at the overwhelming postpartum pain and vulnerability that overcomes you. No one told you about that.

The tears you shed during your recovery and the twenty different emotions you feel at the same time confuse you and set the tone for a journey that begins with self-doubt. *Am I doing this right? Am I doing enough? Am I enough?*

The days feel like a week, and the nights feel like a month. Your mind tries to understand how this body that feels foreign is still yours. Everything is such a blur that you don't look in the mirror for days, and when you accidentally pass one, you weep. You don't recognize your own reflection.

No one told you about that.

As the long weeks pass, you hear that first giggle. You cry. You cry because that tiny, gentle, innocent giggle means you must be doing something right. Your heart bursts with pride and joy, and this time the tears mean you might be just enough.

You watch that sweet angel develop and learn and grow and become a person. A *person*. Somehow, you were part of that.

All that baby wants is you. They crave your smell, your voice, your presence, your touch. *You.* How special is that? Even on your bad days. Even on the days when everything is a disaster and your whole life feels like a pile of failures.

Nothing gets done, yet you haven't stopped working all day and night. On those days, you fall apart on the bathroom floor and ask God for His grace to be poured into your life because you just can't anymore.

No one told you about that.

You persist in this never-ending cycle of feeding, cleaning, shushing, gazing, waking up, changing, checking on their breathing, bathing, washing, cleaning, and cleaning again and again and again.

And then you blink.

Now they're running around, joking about poop, and spilling their juice boxes all over the new couch. They tell you they love you. They throw tantrums at the grocery store. They rest their heads on your chest. They put stickers all over your face. They miss you when you're gone for ten minutes. You, mama, are their world.

Now you cut their snacks into stars because you know they'll eat it that way. You reread their favorite book every night. You've figured that if you turn on *Bubble Guppies* and run to the bathroom, you'll have exactly three minutes and forty-eight seconds to take your shower, and you *know* you'll end up brushing your teeth while holding them.

And now you really don't mind it.

Your arm muscles have gotten so strong from holding them all day that you're kind of proud when you flex them in the mirror. You overhear them saying they want to fly to the moon or change the world. You notice them developing a taste for music or taking an interest in insects.

They are kind to people, and they offer help to their classmates. They respect others. They show compassion.

You've made them feel confident and told them they're brave. You've brushed their hair and told them they could be whatever they wanted to be. You've protected them, soothed them, comforted them.

These kids are the fruit of a labor of love. You repeated yourself over and over and over again. And even though it didn't seem like it, it worked.

I'm guessing you know what I mean. You've discovered this new person inside you. You didn't break. You bent backward, forward, and to all sides. You picked yourself up off the floor, and you showed up. Some days with a lollipop stuck to the back of your hair, and some days with gluten-free homemade treats.

Some days the floors were so clean you could see your reflection in them. Some days you had to wear the ugly underwear because the laundry basket was overflowing.

You learned you're resilient. You're strong. You're creative and capable and kind.

You nurtured them, and they nurtured you. You are a powerful, unstoppable force.

On the days you feel like you're failing, remember that. Remember they're here because of you. They'll never forget the way you made them feel safe. They'll remember how you apologized after you yelled about stepping on the toys you asked them a thousand times to clean up. They'll remember the fort you built in the living room using all your clean sheets, the ones you had to rewash after.

You're doing it right.

You let them see you cry and laugh and worry and rejoice, because they need to learn they're human and will feel all these emotions too.

Do you love and admire that woman now? I do.

Because she *is* enough, after all. You were supposed to be their mother. No one else.

And you are . . . *enough*.

Maya Vorderstrasse is a mom of three, who loves being raw and honest about the wonderful and the challenging parts of motherhood. You are not alone!

You Showed Me the Way

JENNIFER THOMPSON

There's so much I would say to you if you were here today. There's so much I would show you. So much I would ask.

It's been more than a decade since you took your last breath in that hospital room, with your husband and your parents by your side while your children slept in the hotel nearby.

I left the hospital the night before, after holding your hand and telling you how much I loved you and what you meant to me. As the tears slipped steadily and silently down my cheeks, a part of me knew I would never see you again. Another part of me didn't want to believe it.

You were my best friend for so long.

You were the first friend I met in the small Indiana town we moved to after my parents divorced. I was a ball of sadness, nerves, and excitement as I sat on the curb at the end of the driveway thinking about the start of the school year. Then I saw you riding down the road perched atop your friend's handlebars, your mess of thick, curly auburn hair blowing in the wind. You were so beautiful. So daring.

The bike skidded to a stop. I was amazed you managed to stay on.

My life felt shattered and uncertain. And you embodied the opposite—you were put together and confident.

I knew in an instant we would be friends. And your smile and invitation to hang out sometime confirmed my hunch to be true.

God brought you into my life exactly when I needed you.

And there you remained until that day in May, when at the age of thirty-one, with so much life yet to live, you took your final breath.

It still feels surreal that you're gone. I wonder if you knew how much you taught me, how much you meant to me.

At seventeen, you gave birth to your first baby and taught me what it meant to be a warrior. You weren't going to let obstacles or statistics keep you from your dreams. You got married and moved into an apartment and made it your home.

I used to come over after school and look around in amazement at the life you were creating. I watched you care for your baby while toys and diapers and other items so foreign to my life lay scattered all around. You talked about your job and your home and all you had planned for the future.

I was a wild kid in high school, and you were all I hoped to be. You never seemed to tire of my stories or my lack of responsibility at a time when your life demanded it. You would talk about being up all night with your son; I would talk about being up all night at a party.

Our lives were so different, but it didn't matter. You were always there. Always welcoming. Always inviting. Always accepting. Always loving. Always encouraging. Always giving.

When we weren't living near each other, we wrote letters. We were in each other's weddings. We cried together and laughed a lot.

Eventually I settled down, and our lives became more similar. I got married, and a year after you gave birth to your third baby, I gave birth to my first.

You gave me hand-me-down sleep sacks, swings, and bouncy seats. You advised me to never buy a wipe warmer because I would regret it. You shared your experience as a mom and gently guided me into motherhood with your wisdom and encouragement and prayers and companionship.

I imagined our kids growing up and all the ways we would be there for each other . . . just like we'd been since the day you came barreling down that road perched atop the handlebars.

After you got sick, you often drove two hours for medical appointments in my city and brought your son, who was just a year older than my daughter, to play. Those overnight trips are some of my fondest memories.

I still have the pair of Elmo slippers you brought my girl. Your son had a matching pair, and they ran around on the back deck, laughing and playing while we talked. You taught me the best way to bake chicken, and we debated over whether rinsing it first was really necessary.

No matter how much your illness changed your physical appearance, it couldn't change you. If anything, you became stronger. More faithful. More determined.

Even as they cut off your beautiful curls in preparation for chemo, you were brave. I watched the hair fall to the ground, one after the other. *Snip. Snip. Snip.* And once again I remembered you on the handlebars, that hair flying in the wind.

You wrote letters to your sons, just in case the bone marrow transplant didn't go as planned. Just in case you didn't make it. We both decided not to believe that. We were going to lean into hope. And we did.

You taught me how to pray in the midst of struggle. How to continue to give when your world is crumbling. How to keep your head up and hold on to hope even in the darkest of times. How to let yourself fall apart and cry big tears and face the impossible. How to say goodbye when you can't imagine what that means. How to love God with all your heart and soul. How to cling to joy. How to beat the odds. How to be a wife and a mother and a friend.

Days before you died, when we were talking on the phone, as we often did, you told me about the garage sale you were having and the tumble you took down the driveway. You told me about your boys and asked about my two girls and my morning sickness. I was pregnant with my third baby—we were both so excited to meet her.

Only you never did.

Her middle name is yours. My best friend. My Emily.

Jennifer Thompson writes at *Truly Yours, Jen* and hopes her words will feel warm, encouraging, inviting, and honest, like receiving a letter from a friend.

Dear Mom,
I Get It Now

EMILY SOLBERG

I used to wonder why my mom was always the last one out of the house.

Without fail, the rest of the family would be waiting impatiently in the car, necks craned toward the front door, counting the minutes on the dashboard clock and willing her to hurry up already.

Heaven forbid if someone didn't get the keys from her first and we found ourselves huddled outside the minivan, hands shoved deep in the pockets of our hoodies, slumping the full weight of our bodies against its silver bulk in protest. What in the world was taking her so long?

Back then, I thought it was because she took forever to get ready. I had a sneaking suspicion she didn't want to go out in public without her makeup on, even though I couldn't imagine why a mom would care so much, really. I pictured her going through her closet, hot rollers still in her hair, deliberating over which pair of high-waisted jeans to wear while we languished in purgatory. I figured she sometimes procrastinated until the last minute. Or perhaps she purposely enjoyed keeping us waiting. Or maybe for some reason she thought right before we were supposed to leave was the perfect time to call Grandma.

I only recently discovered the truth, now that I'm a mom myself.

While the rest of us waited, Mom was throwing one last load of laundry in the dryer. Picking up a discarded shoe from the middle of the hallway. Packing picnic lunches. Making sure the basement light was off. Refilling the dog's water bowl. Grabbing extra towels, just in case. Searching through the junk drawer to find a coupon for the ice cream place. Making a note to pick up more orange juice. Taking a hot minute to use the bathroom by herself for a change. And yes, maybe even dabbing on a bit of lipstick.

When she finally appeared, pulling on her jacket in a one-woman balancing act while holding keys and pocketbook and travel mug, she was always met with an exasperated, "Come onnnnn, Mom!"

She responded by shooting daggers at us from her eyes.

I get it now. My mom wasn't the last person out the door because she was slow or lazy or inefficient with her time. She wasn't distracted or disorganized. She wasn't procrastinating. She wasn't overly concerned about her appearance.

It was because she loved us so well. Even when we didn't notice. Even when we were ungrateful. Even when we didn't understand. Now I do.

She loved us so well that she took care of absolutely everyone and everything else before she took care of herself. Because that's just what moms do.

Emily Solberg is a mom of two, soldier, and MilSpouse. She supports moms in their parenting journeys and shares her own over at *Shower Arguments*.

Lessons Learned at the Bus Stop

REBECCA HASTINGS

✕

Are other parents doing the same thing? I wondered as I stood in the cold with my fourth grader. For a moment I thought she might be too old for me to be doing this. I've seen some of her friends at the bus stop alone. Maybe I was making the wrong call. Maybe I was holding on too tight.

As I watched the big yellow bus pull to a stop, my girl kissed me and walked up the steps to the very back row. The fourth graders are the seniors of elementary school, and they get to sit in the back. She was cool. Still, she waved.

I smiled and waved back as the bus pulled away. Not the long, enthusiastic wave of a kindergarten parent. No, this was the short wave and nostalgic smile of a parent who feels the days slipping through her fingers.

The clock is ticking an invisible countdown to more independence for both of us. It makes me both excited and sad. I'm holding the clock's hands, willing them to stay still and to move forward. If only I could make them stop for a moment longer, to enjoy this stage. To savor the moments, the way people told me to when my babies were little and I just wanted to sleep. I never understood how right they were. Yet here I am again, pressing forward into all the new things to come.

I want yesterday and today and tomorrow. I want to hold them all in my hands so I can have every piece of who my kids are. As I watch my youngest ride away on the bus, I know the last bus stop days are coming.

I'm grateful I can see this ending coming. So many others truly are invisible. You never know when it will be the last time your little one comes into your bed at night after a bad dream or the final time your daughter asks you to help with her hair. You won't see the last 2 a.m. rocking session coming through your bleary eyes. Of course, you also won't see the last time you'll be spit up on. One makes you want to hold on; the other brings unrecognized celebration.

You won't know the last book you'll read to them, snuggled under the covers and lost in imaginary lands, or the final time your taxi service is needed for rides to school or sports or friends' houses.

We think about the firsts, marking them as milestones on video and in photos. They are exciting and new, but the lasts can be just as beautiful. Both have the ability to take your breath away. And perhaps the lasts are even more poignant, because while they are celebratory, they are also a memorial of sorts in your heart.

No one warns you those first steps you capture on video will eventually lead your baby up the steps to the back of the bus, to school, to work, to a family, and to a life all their own.

Even if they had warned you, you wouldn't understand until you watched it happen. It's something you need to live to know. If someone tells you too early, you'll simply nod and smile, perhaps making a quip about how you won't miss the midnight feedings or the temper tantrums or the teen angst.

As parents, we know we can't be two places at once. This process of becoming is no exception. So we keep moving forward, into a land of the unknown. There's nothing we can do to stop it, but we can choose to see it, to be aware of the ordinary moments that matter. We can hold on to today and breathe it in . . . even on hard days. Yes, there are things we'll be glad to see go, like diapers and homework battles and endless driving and fights to eat one bite of vegetables. But in the middle of all those things, there are the ones we'll miss.

So I'll stand at the bus stop as long as she'll let me, holding on to today with tomorrow just a step away.

Rebecca Hastings, a wife and mom of three in Connecticut, is often found typing words, driving her kids places, or wherever there is chocolate.

Jesus,
My Baby,
and Me

LIZ SPENNER

✕

The desperate thought surged through me without warning, threatening to break my entire being. Baby number four moved within my growing belly as I tried to muffle hot, hysterical tears.

That was the night my anxiety and depression set out to win, one final time. I almost gave up the battle there on the floor, with my back against our king-size bed. It was a bed that housed hundreds of memories: toddler giggles, sick nights, jumps, and flips. A bed that every night heard the quiet prayers of my anxious mama heart.

The weather that late-fall evening night was rainy and cool. Tears began to soak my shirt right where two little feet were quietly exploring inside.

The weight of the entire world was on my chest as two liars came barreling in like thieves in the night—anxiety and depression. They filled my overwhelmed heart and anxious mind with the most pressing lies yet.

Goodness, I was tired. Tired of it all. So tired I was ready to give up.

Maybe He will just forgive me and let us be together. Maybe God will see the good I've done and let us be together in heaven, this baby girl and me, I thought.

I knew she deserved better. I was already falling to pieces, and she wasn't even born yet. So beautifully strong and purposeful, this little being was.

But anxiety and depression told me their biggest lie of all: that the world would be a better place without me and my baby. No doubt my husband and three other precious daughters would be better off too.

Deep within my heart, I knew this wasn't true. But the lies persuaded me otherwise.

So I did the only thing I could think to do, the only thing left to do in such a moment. I cried out to my heavenly Father. A broken, muffled, whispered scream. Through the tears. Through the pressure in my chest. Through the fear and the breathlessness. I needed Him more than ever.

With every ounce of energy I could muster, I begged Him to hold me and my precious baby girl right there on the bedroom floor. To place His sheltering wings around us and fight with us and for us.

Then I felt those little legs inside me move harder, and I knew God was telling us, *You are worth it.* I went to the bathroom to wash the tears from my face, and in the mirror, I saw the eyes of a mother teetering between complete despair and overwhelming relief.

And that's when I saw it: the face of Jesus overshadowing my own, looking back at me in the glow of the bathroom nightlight. The rest of the house was asleep. It was just my Savior, my baby, and me.

I began to imagine every tiny detail of my baby's precious face. Her smile. Her eyes. Her sweet newborn scent.

And my heart knew there was no way I could miss the moment we would meet face to face, eye to eye, heart to heart. My tiny hero, finally in my arms.

There's no doubt in my mind Jesus put us to bed extra carefully that night. He knelt down and kissed us both, tucking us in at the very same spot I'd been breaking into pieces and begging for His strength, presence, and protection only moments before. In His unconditional embrace, He gently reminded me we were not done. Together we had so much to live for—the three of us.

Each of us has a story to share. Maybe you're drowning in overwhelming waves of anxiety and depression yourself. But you are made in His image. You, too, have a beautiful, one-of-a-kind purpose. You, too, can find courage, faith, and hope in Him.

One day I will share my story with my daughter. How Jesus used her tiny, unborn feet to remind me of my purpose in Him. How He pieced me back together on the darkest night of my life.

And how we live for a God who is stronger than the lies of despair.

Liz Spenner is a Christian motherhood writer and blogger who lives in the Midwest with her wonderful husband, six beautiful children, and energetic boxer dog.

Lessons in Motherhood
from Row 19, Seat B

JENNI BRENNAN

✕

19B. That's where she sat for four long hours: row 19, seat B, while I sat in row 23, seat F.

She was one of those airport strangers you keep seeing throughout your travel day. And over the course of just a few hours, she became someone I would remember forever.

19B was a version of me from long ago, one that existed before my long, dark hair turned gray and my forehead developed permanent wrinkles. She was a version of me that existed back when my teenagers were babies and toddlers. Watching her was like stepping back in time.

"How am I going to do this?" she muttered to herself earlier in the day as she maneuvered through the airport with car seats, strollers, a baggage cart, and two small boys in tow. With determination in her eyes and a no-nonsense attitude, she was a force to be reckoned with. But it was obvious she was also exhausted and overwhelmed, teetering on the edge of a breakdown.

So many moms have been 19B, sweating as we make our way through an airport, desperate to get home and return to the mundane yet comforting routine of life with small children.

As I stood in line behind her, waiting for my turn to hand over my luggage to the airline employee, I remembered what it was like to be that mom. Back then, traveling with young children was a marathon that required an almost infinite number of tools: bottles, formula, breast pumps, diapers, extra clothes, baby food, blankies, teethers, soft toys, car seats, strollers, folding cribs, and various medicines for "just in case" moments. There were no breaks. There were no rests. Every moment of a travel day centered on finding a way to balance everyone's needs and get where we were going without leaving anyone or anything behind.

It was exhausting to be 19B.

I swore I'd never miss those days, but as I stood in that long line, my heart ached just a bit. I missed when my own boys were tinier versions of themselves, with their raspy little voices calling to me from their stroller, just as 19B's did, saying, "Mama, need help."

I turned to face my own two boys, both old enough to tower above me now. They no longer complain about long lines or ask toddler questions like "How much longer, Mama?" when we travel. Instead, they happily tap away on their phones as they play games, scroll social media, and talk to their friends miles away. Every once in a while, they look up and make eye contact with me and even sometimes engage in an actual conversation.

My teens don't need me to escort them to the bathroom. They don't need me to order their snacks. They don't need me to bring along a Mary Poppins bag filled with entertainment. They don't even need me to pack their bags. They don't need me like they used to. They are almost entirely self-sufficient. They are everything I wished for when I was 19B.

But in that moment, I missed when they needed me more.

As I watched 19B walk toward her gate with one of her little sidekicks beside her, my heart ached again. Even though it always slowed us down, there was something so innocent and endearing when one of my boys would insist on pulling his own suitcase, determined to do it "all by myself," only to grow tired and look at me, just as 19B's son did, and say, "Mama, need help."

Mama, need help. Oh how I miss those words!

Although the plane was mostly dark during our nighttime flight, I could see and hear 19B tending to her boys almost nonstop. They were hungry. They were tired. They were bored. They wanted to get up. They wanted to be done.

Four rows behind her, in seat 23F, I was having a much different flight experience. My boys each had their own headphones, ordered their own food, and kept themselves busy. I was free to nap, finish an entire movie, or just sit in silence. No one needed me. It was somehow both lovely and lonely.

When the plane landed, I watched as 19B maneuvered her overhead luggage while corralling her children into the aisle and toward the front of the plane.

"Mom, need help?" my oldest called to me, pulling my attention away from 19B. He pointed to my own carry-on bag above me.

I smiled and nodded, mouthing, "Thank you."

The "Mama, need help" of my 19B days has now become, "Mom, need help?" Same nouns. Same verb. Completely different meanings. 19B versus 23F.

As I stepped into the aisle, I couldn't help but catch the eye of an older woman a few rows back in 26C. Her eyes shifted to my oldest son and back to me, a soft smile on her face. Clearly she had witnessed his offer of help. I wondered if she had been watching me with my boys the way I had been watching 19B, feeling a nostalgic pull toward what used to be.

That's what we do so often as moms, right? We survive, and when we have a spare moment, we reflect. We rush through the airport, efficiently and expertly meeting everyone's needs along the way. And then one day we lift our eyes and realize seasons have changed, years have passed, and we are now seated somewhere completely different in life.

This is motherhood. It's the almost constant push and pull between wanting to move forward to the next stage and wanting to go back to the way it used to be. It's the act of yearning for the earlier times while trying to survive in the present and find hope for the future. It's finding the beauty in every seat.

Even row 19, seat B.

Jenni Brennan is a grief therapist, college professor, and podcaster. She is the founder of *Changing Perspectives* online and author of *Confessions From the Couch*.

Goodbye, Jean

SARAH LUKE

On the day we met them, she wore lavender pants and her husband shuffled along behind her. Her name was Jean, and his name was Dale, and they bought the house next door. Soon after they moved in, our boys discovered Jean liked to bake cookies and Dale liked to sit on the deck to watch the kids play. They became part of our lives, and we became part of theirs. They refused to install underground sprinklers, telling me they could move a lot of hoses around for two thousand dollars. Many mornings, I saw Jean moving her sprinklers before we finished breakfast.

A few months after they moved into the neighborhood, Dale fell and was never the same. But he always came home from the hospital, and Jean always took care of him. She was a self-reliant lady, and I rarely saw her armor crack.

Eventually, Jean could no longer care for Dale. A few months after her eightieth birthday, she moved him to the VA hospital. For thirteen months, she visited him almost every day, making sure his care was up to her standards.

One morning my doorbell rang, and there was Jean. Dale had passed away during the night, and we cried together.

By then, I had met most of her family members. We talked about the funeral arrangements, and I hid my smile when she told me Dale's aunt wouldn't be there because of her health. Dale was eighty-five—how old could his aunt be?

As a widow, Jean stayed in her home and kept busy. She installed floor trim, built covers for egress windows, painted every room in the house, and hung a suspended ceiling throughout the basement. I frequently saw her using power tools in her garage. This same lady wore pink curlers and a bathrobe while hanging her laundry to dry.

She covered the base of her tomato plants with eggshells and coffee grounds. She put shredded paper over the roots of her tiny pine trees, telling me how good it was for them. We exchanged cucumbers and tomatoes, her yield consistently outpacing mine. She liked to let me know when our dog was up to no good. Sometimes I think her view of our yard might have been too good.

Jean liked to knock on my garage door when she wanted to come in and chat. Many times she invited the kids and me over for coffee and cookies when I knew I should be making supper. She seemed to know there was always one more thing to do—better to take time for coffee and cookies while you can.

Eventually, Jean put her house up for sale to move closer to friends. We were happy for her but sad for us. She offered us some of her furniture, including a couch, a bathroom cabinet, a snow blower, a microwave, and tomato cages. Her eyes teared up as she made her plans, and I could tell her armor was cracking just a little. She gave us all these things, but she gave us so much more by being the neighbor she was—she and Dale both.

One day I saw Jean shoveling the mountain of snow in her driveway. I joined her, and we cleared a path for her vehicle. She loaded up the last of her belongings but wouldn't tell me when she was leaving for good. I tried to give back the house key she'd once given me, but she refused to take it.

When I saw Jean's vehicle a few days later, I went over to say goodbye. There was no answer, so I let myself in. The house was empty. Just a coffee percolator and one mug remained on the counter. I stood there for a minute, remembering all the times I'd been there with the boys, sipping coffee and eating cookies at suppertime.

I left the key on the counter, shut the door, and went home. She wasn't one for emotions, and she never did come back to say goodbye.

Many years later, the new neighbors welcomed a baby girl into their family. Her middle name?

Jean.

Sarah Luke raises sons with her husband and writes the stories of their lives to keep forever in her heart.

I Am the Everyday Dishes of My Family

MARALEE BRADLEY

I am the family's everyday dishes.

No one has ever described me as "dainty" or "precious." I am hardy and used to withstanding heat and pressure. I am not saved for special occasions.

I am the daughter who came home. I'm the local girl who will bring the green beans when the relatives come back for a visit. I'm not the one you plan around or schedule out in advance. I am the last-minute, the "Oh, by the way," the "If you don't mind." I am the one who drops by, who brings extra tomatoes from her garden, who knows how everybody's kids are doing in school and when my dad is away on business.

I am the mother who stays home. I don't return from somewhere exciting to be met with hugs and exclamations of joy. I am the everyday mom who is there when you wake up each morning and there to put you to bed at night.

I'm the constant in a changing world. During each season of motherhood, from the diapers to the driver's license, I will be the same. I will be present until I am almost forgettable. I am not new and shiny. I'm the creator of routines, the keeper of the chore chart, the reason we are all sane, which some days costs me a little of my own sanity.

I am the faithful wife. Each day, a little older, a little grayer, a little wiser, and a little less gullible. I'm here when you get home, with a hot meal on the table, remnants of the day's lipstick barely clinging to my lips. I keep the laundry managed and the bathrooms clean, and I wonder if you see me anymore. My adventures are small—a trip to the library, lunch with friends, a church event. Will you care about them when I tell you? Will you see them the way I do, or will they look like the unimportant escapades of a bored housewife?

I am the everyday dishes of my family. But I don't resent it.

I am the one you can count on to be present in a crisis. I'm not too fragile for your problems. I'm familiar and faithful enough to be trusted with any job and every joy. I've seen you at your worst, and I've loved you at your best. I've been a witness to it all, because I've been here through it all. I haven't been spared or saved or hidden away. I'm chipped and stained and glued back together from the hardships I've seen. But I'm strong.

The fine china never knows the joy of the mundane—a happiness I've become familiar with. To be ever-present means being there for the first steps, the first words, the first love notes, and the first locker combinations. I haven't missed a thing, and I've cherished it all in my heart. I've noticed the subtle changes in your demeanor when the day has been hard, and I scramble to make it right. I know the recipes you love and when you need a minute to yourself or a night with friends. I stay just above the chaos, coordinating, managing, swimming with my head barely above the surface.

I don't regret being the everyday dishes. There's a place for the fancy and fine, but that's not me. I can appreciate the beauty of those who haven't been broken by this world, and I sometimes wish for a life I wasn't given or maybe never really wanted—a life of adventure or a life being precious. Instead, I find joy in being dependable and predictable.

I rest in the confidence that my mother knows I will come when there's a crisis and I will always bring the green beans. I'm thankful my kids know I'm fully present, I'm near when they need me, and I'm cheering them on when they don't. I will be content knowing my husband sees me as his closest friend and trusts me with an intimacy he doesn't share with anyone else. And I will continue to invest in myself with a value on growing and learning while also embracing who I love to be.

I don't need to invent dreams I'm supposed to follow. I don't have to become a superwoman version of myself to be worthy of love. I don't need to do more or be more to prove I have value. I can be the everyday dishes of my family. And that's enough for me.

Maralee Bradley is a wife, mother of eight, writer, speaker, and passionate advocate for kids.

Love the People
in Your Own Backyard

CAROLYN MOORE

×

"We could have went yesterday," my daughter said through a mouthful of waffles this morning.

"Gone," I automatically corrected, throwing an expectant look at her across the table.

"Gone, gone, gone," she parroted with a sigh. "We could have gone yesterday."

I nodded approvingly as my husband rolled his eyes with a smirk. He knows the drill—everyone in our house does—and he knew what would come out of my mouth next.

"You'll thank me for it one day."

When my brothers and I were growing up, our mom employed the exact same (possibly excessively strict) grammar correction method. Any time one of us uttered a *went* instead of a *gone* or a *seen* instead of a *saw*, we had to say the right word three times, then repeat the sentence correctly.

We, too, would roll our eyes and groan as she insisted we'd thank her for it when we were adults with perfect grammar. Then we grew up and realized she'd been right—and started doing the same thing to our kids.

Isn't that just how it goes with a mom? She says things and makes you do things that, at the time, seem silly or useless or empty. Then you get a little older and realize just how right she was.

Teenage me would be cringing, I'm sure, but even she would admit it's the truth. And it turns out Mom was right about a lot of things, not just pronouns and participles. Now that I'm a mother, I find myself replaying a lot of my mom's oft-repeated advice in my head.

"It's good to have options," she'd say when I was facing a decision that felt paralyzing.

"You'll know what to do," she'd reassure me when I was doubtful or over-thinking something.

And my favorite, the one I keep tucked away in a corner of my heart for easy reference when life feels heavy and hard, when I'm trying to do and be all the things: "Go home and love the people in your own backyard."

I have to remind myself of that often these days, when so many voices are vying for my attention and energy and care. And so many of those voices exist outside the four walls of my greatest influence and most important mission field: home.

Because something happens to us when we become mothers—we try to do it all, all the time, for all the people, and do it all *right*.

We look for the safest car seats for our babies long before they're ever born. We make birth plans and practice tummy time and plan out reasonable nap schedules and adequate feedings. We research developmental milestones and pea-nut allergies and suspicious rashes. We worry over teaching shapes and making the *th* instead of the *f* sound and practice basic manners.

We watch our children grow and change and gain the sort of independence that simultaneously thrills and devastates us. We feel them pull away and come into their own and cling to the hope they'll come back to us one day.

We pray while they sleep. We ache when they hurt. We cheer (and worry a tiny bit) when they soar.

And sometimes, we simply forget.

Those teenagers sitting at the kitchen counter in fuzzy socks mindlessly scroll-ing on their phones.

Those school-aged kids who only stop moving long enough to shovel in a few bites of macaroni and cheese.

Those toddlers who test our limits and try our patience with their toothy grins and boundless curiosity.

Those babies who depend on us for literal life and make us lose sleep and grow bigger hearts.

They are *yours*. Yours to teach and nurture and raise. Yours to influence and learn from and cry over. Yours to annoy with grammar lessons that will make them roll their eyes and know in their very bones just how much you care.

They are the people in your own backyard, the borrowed souls in your sanctuary of space and time—and you get to love them.

You write your story together, a beautifully unique masterpiece sparkling with laughter and tears and a million little moments that go by in a blink. It's probably simple, sometimes exhausting, and undoubtedly filled with mistakes (sorry, Mom) that make it your own.

And that story? It matters. Because they matter. Because you matter. Because this life you're living matters to the One who made you a mother.

And that is simply everything.

Carolyn Moore serves as editor in chief of *Her View From Home* and is a wife and mom of five in the Midwest.

Conclusion

LESLIE MEANS

✕

I almost quit. Scratch that—I did quit. It got too hard. It broke me. I couldn't do it anymore.

Her View From Home wasn't making any money. I didn't have enough to pay myself, let alone the writers or our web developers. I was exhausted. And lonely. And sad. And defeated.

I cried myself to sleep that night, knowing in the morning, I would shut it all down.

But morning came, and His whispers were clear. *Don't quit. Keep going.*

It's weird to say I heard God talking to me. People have asked, "How did you know it was God?"

And honestly? I can't explain it. It wasn't an audible voice (although that would be cool and terrifying, but mostly cool), but I just knew.

The next few months were tough, but I didn't give up. Many nights I would lie in bed begging God for answers.

"Please take this from my shoulders, God."

"Please lead me in the right direction."

"Please explain to me why you want me to keep this website going."

My husband and I refinanced our home, which gave us one month without a mortgage payment. One month to make it work.

And then we found out we were expecting our third baby. Any normal person with a broke business and a small human on the way would call it quits and get a steady, reliable job.

But God didn't make me a normal person, I suppose. The whispers became shouts, and I just knew it would be okay. I had so much unexplainable peace.

A new email came in not long after that.

"Leslie, I've prayed about it, and I really want to share my friend's story on your website," the stranger wrote.

Let's put this into perspective: at this point, *Her View From Home* had about 18,000 Facebook followers. We were small. How did this woman find us? I'm still not sure, but I think God had something to do with it.

The story she wanted us to share was a powerful piece about her friend who, at four months postpartum, died by suicide.

It was heartbreaking and gut wrenching and raw. But this woman knew her friend's story would save lives.

And it did. Her story went viral.

Another email came a few days later. "Thank you for sharing this story," the stranger said. "It saved my life."

"Okay, God—I hear you," I told Him. *Her View From Home* had a greater purpose—one much bigger than me—and I would do everything I could to keep it going.

Her View From Home was never the same after that day. Writers and readers from across the globe found us. Story after story and whisper after whisper kept the site going. Today we have an incredible writing community and a staff of women dedicated to sharing stories that change lives. And we have this book.

Maybe *So God Made a Mother* didn't turn out to be the book you were expecting when you picked it up. Honestly? It didn't turn out to be the book our team was expecting either. It's so much more.

The stories on these pages aren't all easy to read. Plenty of them highlight the happiness and joy of motherhood, but many of them show the hard, heavy parts too. But that's exactly what being a mom is, you know?

It's beautiful—and hard.

It's rewarding—and exhausting.

It's joyous—and devastating.

As we wove together this book, we realized telling the whole story—not just the feel-good highlight reel—was part of its purpose. You deserve to hear the whole story. Because friend, we're all so much more than just the pretty parts. And sometimes the hard parts are where we find the real beauty of this motherhood journey.

I wish I could be sitting across from you now over a cup of coffee or some good cheese, talking about what you've just read, about the pieces that stood out to both of us and why. Stories are such a powerful way to relate to one another, and we need those connections with other women so much, especially these days.

My hope is this book helps you do just that. I hope somewhere in these pages you see yourself and the incredible way God is authoring your story, no matter what chapter you're in.

If I had ignored His whispers all those years ago, the book you're holding wouldn't be a reality. The thought of it brings me to my knees. God is so cool. Maybe His whispers were meant for you, friend. Maybe He told me to keep going so you would read the words on these pages.

Your story is important. You are a unique part of God's perfect plan. Wherever you are, whatever you do, whoever you come from, your story matters. I'm sure of it.

Don't ever be afraid to share it.

Afterword

Like so many other women, I was an incredible mother *before* I had kids. By that I mean: my invisible, hypothetical children—the tiny humans who existed in my head before they existed in the flesh—slept ten hours a night, ate their vegetables without complaint, and of course, *never* disobeyed.

My husband is the youngest of three boys, and more than once, I've heard my mother-in-law refer to her second son as a "humility child." Her firstborn fed her ego; he was compliant, cautious, and highly responsible. "Then along came Kevin," she jokes. "And I realized I had no idea what I was doing as a parent."

Looking back on my first decade of motherhood, I believe two things have humbled me as a mom: (1) the process of actually raising children, and (2) reading hundreds (thousands?) of stories from fellow mothers.

It's easy to view hypothetical parenthood in absolutes before you're required to live out the nuances of reality. I'm embarrassed to tell you how many opinions I held tightly—about birth, breastfeeding, screen time—before I ever saw two lines on a pregnancy test. And while my firstborn, Everett, turned out to be a relatively easy baby, I'd still say he humbled me real quick.

Like Leslie and the other beautiful writers who contributed to this collection, I write to make sense of everything swirling around me—the ups, the downs, the joys, the heartaches. As someone who runs a storytelling community for women, I have a whole new appreciation for the power of storytelling.

While it's easy to view all of parenthood through the microscope of our own experiences, I find that when we open our eyes and ears and hearts to the stories of other women, it helps us zoom out. Stories can paint a vivid picture of a situation we've never had to think about or endure. Stories call us to consider what it would be like to face infertility, loss, adoption, a difficult diagnosis, or trauma, even if we've never walked through any of those specific circumstances ourselves.

Stories have the power to move us, stir us, and make us feel something profound. Stories have a way of cracking us open a bit and breaking down our absolutes, our black-and-white thinking, our tightly held opinions over choices that may or may not actually be available—or best—for everyone. Stories propel us into the real world with more empathy, more compassion, more kindness, more love.

This book is a gift, not just because it's filled with honest prose and entertaining anecdotes, but because reading these pages expands our view of what motherhood is and what motherhood can be. Bearing witness to these stories will no doubt stretch our hearts, soften us, and arm us with grace and mercy as we catch another mother's eye across the aisle in Target, at the soccer field, or in the hospital waiting room.

As you close this book, I beg you to tuck these stories into your heart, and then write your own. Use this collection as a jumping-off point, a nudge to walk through the world, as Leslie says at the beginning of this book, with "breathtaking vulnerability."

Here's to the stories we have yet to read and the stories waiting to be written. And of course, here's to the awesome kids, our forever muses, who keep us humble along the way.

Ashlee Gadd
Founder of Coffee + Crumbs and author of Create Anyway:
The Joy of Pursuing Creativity in the Margins of Motherhood

Acknowledgments

I'll say it forever: I couldn't have done it without this team.

To Carolyn, the best editor in the history of ever. Your name should be on this book. Thank you for believing in this mission. Thank you for believing in me. It's bigger than us, friend. #6hours. To Casey, you have the best eye for design, and your words are solid gold. Thank you for sticking with me and my big dreams. We are blessed to have you. You both have become more than coworkers, more than friends. You're family.

To Kelsey, Emily, Jenny, and Charissa—you are the best team. You dive in and just "do it," even when I'm too frazzled to guide you. Thank you, thank you, thank you.

To Sarah and Kara, thanks for sending that first email, even though I thought you were spam and didn't respond. Oops. But God knew. He always does. Thank you for your gentle guidance and prayers. Thank you for working tirelessly to help us create this beautiful book. To Stephanie and Dean, thank you for crafting these pages into something magical. To the entire Tyndale team, we are honored to partner with you.

To Claudia and Katherine, thank you for being two of the best agents out there. Working with you is a dream.

To Liza, Caitlin, Kelsea, and the AGPR team, thank you for your unending enthusiasm and for helping us go after some of our wildest goals.

To Carolyn's mom and dad, your wisdom got me through some of the hardest days. Everything is not spinning out of control.

To Whitney, Brea, Ashli, Lisa, and Lauren, I'm forever grateful God put you in my path. Thank you—and countless others—for helping us build *Her View From Home*.

To Amy, thank you for that phone call. I'll never forget it. I'm grateful for you. Always.

To Ashlee, thank you for adding your beautiful words to this book. I've looked up to you and your community for years.

To David, Josh, and the entire Control Yours team, I know we're a lot. You know we're a lot. And yet you have the best customer service I've ever experienced. I rest easy at night because I know your team has us covered. Thank you for your tech knowledge. I couldn't do it without you. (But seriously. I couldn't.)

To Bruno, thank you for being another tech genius on our team. I don't know how you create that calendar system, but it's cool. And we're grateful.

To Chip, thank you for being an excellent attorney. I'll recommend you to anyone.

To Sheila, thank you for your encouragement. Money is scary, but it's less so when you're on our side.

To Jan, my first and best female boss. "Build the life you want; you can." You told me that. Thank you for always believing in me.

To our beloved *Her View From Home* writing community and the authors in this book, thank you for trusting us with your stories. We are honored and humbled to publish your words. Always.

To *Her View From Home* readers, thank you for loving us for so long. Your kind words and support have been a source of encouragement since we launched. We're forever grateful for you.

To the residents of central Nebraska, your support in those early days means more than you'll ever know. I would not have been able to launch *Her View From Home* without you. I'm honored to call this place home.

To my sisters, Lora, Lisa, and Lindsay, thank you for always looking out for me, the baby of the family. You helped raise me, and I turned out great. Must be because you had your hand in it. I love you guys.

To Mom and Dad, thank you for the best childhood. Thank you for teaching me that no dream is too big and how to think outside the box. Mostly, thank you for your unconditional love.

To my babies, Ella, Grace, and Keithan, being your mom is and always will be my greatest achievement. I love you.

To Kyle: people often ask how I started *Her View From Home*. How did a farm girl from the middle of the country create this community? The answer is you. It's always been you. You believed in me even when I didn't. No dream was too wild; no goal was too big. You're my safe space, my rock. You're my everything. I love you, forever and ever.

About the Author

✕

Leslie Means is founder and owner of the popular website *Her View From Home*, which features heartfelt contributor stories on motherhood, marriage, faith, and grief. She is a former news anchor and a weekly columnist, and she has published several short stories. She is married to a very patient man named Kyle, and together they have three fantastic kids: Ella, Grace, and Keithan. When she's not sharing too much personal information online or in the newspaper, you'll find her somewhere in Nebraska spending time with family and friends.